D1144702

THE PURE PACKAGE

'The Pure Package recipes are an absolute delight; I loved all of the dishes, it's too difficult to pick just one! The food is extremely healthy, yet you don't feel like you're going without as it is so filling and scrumptious – a real treat! **A lifesaver for tired new mums**.'

DENISE VAN OUTEN

'The Pure Package really helped me get my head around eating healthy food. As a result I'm much more aware about what I put into my body – it gave me a bit of a wake-up call! **I think the food is absolutely fantastic**... I enjoyed knowing that what I was eating was the correct portions of healthily balanced food and **I loved how the food wasn't restricted, bland or boring**.' LISA SNOWDON

'The Pure Package ensured every meal is tasty. The dishes are absolutely delicious, really fresh and visually appealing; I couldn't wait to tuck in each morning!' ALEXANDRA BURKE

'Surprisingly delicious'

OBSERVER

First published in Great Britain in 2012
by Weidenfeld & Nicolson
10 9 8 7 6 5 4 3 2 1

Text © Jennifer Irvine 2012
Design and layout © Weidenfeld & Nicolson 2012

All rights reserved. No part of this publication may be reproduced,
stored in a retrieval system, or transmitted, in any form or by
any means, electronic, mechanical, photocopying, recording or
otherwise, without the prior permission of both the copyright owner
and the above publisher.

The right of Jennifer Irvine to be identified as the author of this
work has been asserted in accordance with the Copyright, Designs
and Patents Act 1988.

A CIP catalogue record for this book is available
from the British Library.

ISBN: 978 0 297 86654 1

Printed and bound in Italy

Commissioning Editor: Amanda Harris
Art Director: Natasha Webber
Designer: Fiona Andreanelli
Food Photographer: Jean Cazals
Stylist: Cynthia Inions
Home Economists: Katie Giovanni, Megan Rogers
    & Julia Azzarello
Editors: Debbie Woska & Nicola Crossley
Proofreader: Ione Walder
Indexer: Cherry Ekins

Weidenfeld & Nicolson
The Orion Publishing Group Ltd
Orion House
5 Upper St Martin's Lane
London WC2H 9EA

An Hachette UK Company

LIBRARIES NI	
C700865604	
RONDO	03/01/2012
613.25	£ 20.00
OMAOMA	

THE PURE PACKAGE

The DIET for FOOD LOVERS

Jennifer Irvine

The Pure Package Philosophy

First of all, I love food. And I also like to look good. And I am busy. So what I need is delicious, healthy and convenient food that will keep my body and mind sharp. Growing up in rural Ireland it was hard not to be inspired by the wonder of growing your own produce and then turning it into something scrumptious. Cooking is my first love! Who would have thought that all those years wearing wellies in the pouring rain, digging for carrots and selling eggs, would lead me here?

From a humble beginning – my kitchen, to be exact – I set out to provide freshly prepared, ethically sourced and tasty yet healthy food. Initially I tested my recipes on my friends, then, concerned that they may just be being polite, I sought out the toughest critics I could find – journalists! The response I got was that everyone loved the food. From there I started making meals for nine clients, which was all the ingredients that my refrigerator could hold!

In 2004, with demand increasing and countless refrigerators and freezers taking over my home, I decided it was time to get help. I moved The Pure Package to the New Covent Garden Market, where I had a wealth of fresh, seasonal produce on my doorstep, I employed a team of chefs, nutritionists and dietary therapists to share the load, and together we designed a range of programmes to cater for people with different needs.

Since then, thousands of people have successfully followed The Pure Package programmes, including celebs like Hugh Jackman, Erin O'Connor and Denise Van Outen – to name just a few! – and time and time again I have been asked by my clients to create a book of our precious recipes. So here it is: the finished article.

I'm so pleased that this means our knowledge and advice is now available to more than just a select few. I hope you love the recipes as much as I do! Feel free to play with the ingredients and make the dishes your own – if you don't like apples but you do like pears then just go for it!

Most of all, enjoy your cooking – it's not just about being healthy, it's about being happy too.

Jennifer Irvine

Founder, *The Pure Package*

Contents

INTRODUCTION

THE PURE PACKAGE IS THE LEADING UK COMPANY of its type to offer freshly prepared, ethically sourced and nutritious meals direct to the doors of people who are primarily time-poor. But even our most loyal clients have periods when their life slows down a little, or they are on holiday, and we have been asked time and time again for a recipe book which will help them to continue this level of wellbeing when they are cooking for themselves.

And then there are the people who are new to The Pure Package, who have the time to cook their own meals, but not the expertise. For those people, too, I hope that this book is an inspiration.

Whatever your lifestyle, eating healthily can be something that becomes part of your daily routine – and this book has been created to help you do just that. Not only is it filled with our most popular dishes, it also sets out our basic principles, giving you all the tools you need to eat correctly and a three-week eating plan to start you off on the right path.

The concept of each recipe is based on food that is good for you, tastes great, and is convenient. For me, food is a friend, not a foe. It is your ally against disease, and so our dishes are designed using the right food in the right quantities. Developed by me, my team and my family, our recipes are put through rigorous tasting sessions before they hit the menu – everyone around our kitchen table has to be excited and dipping in for more before we are happy to take a dish forward… and then hours are spent making sure the carbohydrates, proteins and fats are perfectly balanced. I've said before: the food can't just taste good – it has to be good for you.

Sourcing fresh, seasonal ingredients is important to me, and I would recommend that you try to buy fruits and vegetables that are locally grown and in season, so that they arrive on your table as soon as possible after they have been harvested. Food that looks fresh and vibrant will most certainly have more flavour and better nutritional qualities. It is important to eat with your eyes: you will enjoy your food much more if it looks good. Supporting ethically produced meat and fish is important too – after all, we need to protect our environment for the future.

I hope our recipes break the perception that you have to deny yourself in order to be healthy. Take our chocolate mousse – it is indulgent, it will make you smile and, most importantly, it is good for you!

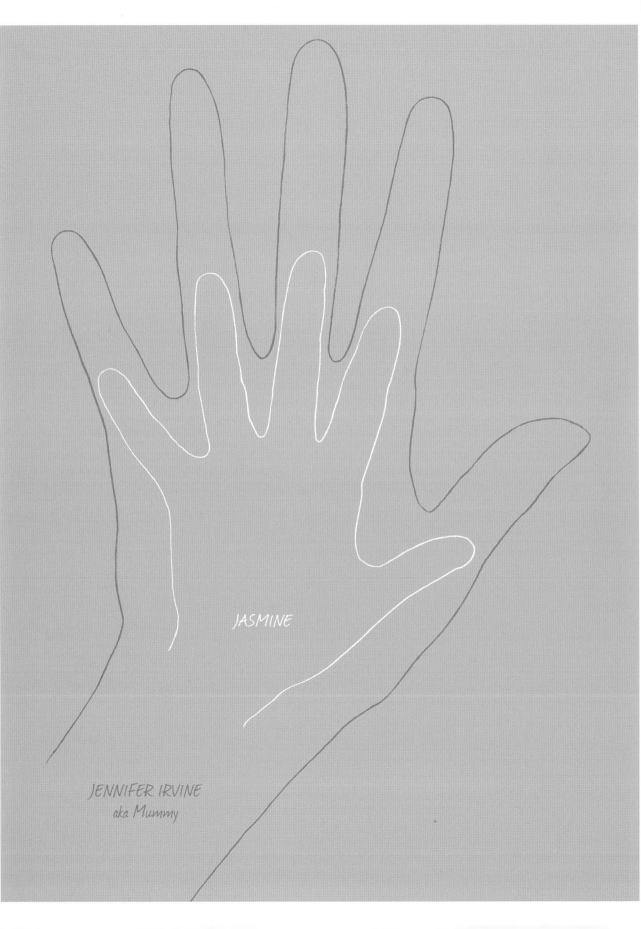

JASMINE

JENNIFER IRVINE
aka Mummy

The Rule of Palm

Let's be real, who has the time to weigh out, measure and portion every meal? I need an easy way to know what the correct portion size is for me using my eyes – and I do this by using the 'rule of palm'.

Eating in the right portions is an important aspect of healthy eating. You could be eating wonderfully healthy food, but still be overweight and lethargic simply because your portions and the balance of key food groups are all wrong. Similarly, if you cut your portions too much and aren't eating enough food, your body will go into 'starvation mode' and will actually start to store fat.

A good general guideline for working out your portion size is by using your own palm. Your meals should always consist of the three key components: protein, complex carbohydrates and fruit and vegetables.

If you are eating a balanced meal then your plate of ingredients should consist of one palm-sized portion of protein, one palm-sized portion of complex carbohydrates and two palm-sized portions of raw or lightly cooked fruit and vegetables.

At The Pure Package we have a team of dietary therapists who have been trained to do mathematical equations based on years of research to figure out exactly how much our clients should be eating. They do this by calculating height, weight and level of exercise and then combining this information with the client's health goals to come up with a recommended portion size. In real life, most people simply do not have the time to do such complicated calculations – and this is where our easy 'rule of palm' fits in. The rule of palm is not an exact science, but it is a super everyday way of calculating your approximate portion size.

The recipes in this book are written in the traditional way, as family dishes for four people. However, it is key when dishing up to think carefully about the 'rule of palm' and how much each family member should be eating. (A really great trick is to trace around your family's hands and stick the templates to the refrigerator. This is fun and gives you an easy reminder of portion sizes.) As you can see opposite, my portions are very different to those of my four-year old daughter.

Using the 'rule of palm' as a guideline will also prevent those dreaded chocolate and crisp cravings as well as helping to combat overeating when you come to sit down for a meal. Savour your food too. In today's rushed society, we often spend all day thinking about what we are going to eat, and then wolf it down in minutes – simply because we haven't eaten correctly that day. This is such a waste. Instead, take your time to enjoy what you are eating. Chew every mouthful. They say it takes 20 minutes for the body to realise you have started eating, so if you finish too soon you may still feel unsatisfied.

Two palm-sized portions of lightly cooked vegetables /fruit
Palm-sized portion of complex carbohydrates
Palm-sized portion of protein

Eat the Rainbow

I mean exactly that. Colourful meals don't just look good on your plate, they ensure you get a variety of vitamins and minerals in your diet, naturally. Most of us are attracted to colour (small children choose their foods by colour before they even know what it is, they want the 'yellow one' or the 'green one') and I find I enjoy my food a lot more if it looks vibrant – there is certainly truth in the saying 'we eat with our eyes'.

Each different colour of fruit or vegetable has a different role in keeping you healthy. For example, purple foods (like berries or grapes) contain flavonoids, powerful antioxidants which help to fight off disease; green foods (such as watercress, broccoli or spinach) are a rich source of magnesium, which is vital for nerve and muscle function; orange foods (carrots, cantaloupe melon, butternut squash) are rich in beta-carotene, which is needed for healthy skin, vision and immune function; red foods (tomatoes, watermelon) are rich in lycopene, an important antioxidant needed to help fight off disease; pink foods (raspberries, strawberries, beetroot) contain anthocyanins, which help control blood pressure and fight bacterial infections.

I always aim to eat five to eight portions of fruit and vegetables a day (the government recommendation is five) and find that the best way to get my multicoloured fix is to make sure that each time I go to the shops or local market my basket contains a rainbow of colours – and the kids love it too.

You will notice our recipes are packed full of an assortment of colourful fruits and vegetables, and unless otherwise specified, they should be left unpeeled. Different parts of fruits and vegetables can enhance the nutritional value of each other, so by eating the skin of the produce not only do you benefit from the skin's nutrients but they in turn can reinforce the pulp's nutritional value as well. The peel is also a rich source of dietary fibre, which aids healthy digestion. Remember to wash your ingredients, especially if using them unpeeled – it's important to remove any dirt and chemical residues that might be on the skin.

I hope my book will encourage you to experiment more with the wonders of fruit and vegetables.

Complex Carbohydrates

Carbohydrates seem to have got a bad name over the last decade, but the right carbs are a vital part of a healthy diet. We need them to fuel all the functions of the body, and the best fuel is complex carbohydrates – the 'browns'.

All carbohydrates are composed of units of sugar, but what differentiates them is the number of units and how they are linked together.

The components of simple carbohydrates (eg. sugar, honey, white flour, white rice) are made of just one or two units, and are quickly digested and released into the bloodstream. Eating these carbs will give you a rush of energy followed by a sudden dip. Not only that, but the body may not use up all the quick-releasing glucose that is produced and so deposits a lot of it for storage as fat.

Complex carbohydrates, as their name suggests, are complex in structure, which means they take longer to digest. Their energy is released slowly into the bloodstream, ensuring that a steady supply of fuel is available to the body over a longer period of time. This is important in maintaining stable blood sugar levels to prevent energy slumps and is a vital consideration in a healthy, balanced diet.

The speed at which the body digests food and converts it to glucose is known as the Glycemic Index (GI) of food. The faster the food is broken down, the higher the rating on the index. It is, however, impractical to memorise the GI rating of every carbohydrate! So, when choosing carbs, a good rule of thumb is to pick those that are as close to their natural form as possible (they are generally brown in colour too). Complex carbs have a lower GI. For example, brown rice has a GI rating of 50, compared to 83 for white rice; traditional oat porridge has a GI of 49 compared to 65 for instant porridge oats.

Where there's not an obvious swap, consider different ingredients, experiment and have fun. Pearl barley (GI of 25) makes a lovely alternative to risotto rice (GI of 69), producing a dish with more bite that has a much lower GI (see our recipe on page 117).

It is not only processing that can affect carbohydrates' GI; the way in which we cook and eat them can also have an effect. New potatoes boiled in their skin provide a more textured bite than peeled mashed potatoes, and have the added bonus of a lower GI (57 rather than 70). I could write a whole book just on carbohydrates and the Glycemic Index, but there are many already out there. There's no need to know all the details – just remember to think brown and think natural. Eating complex carbs will give you sustained energy levels, keep you fuller for longer and prevent hunger pangs and cravings.

All of the recipes in this book have been designed to optimally balance your blood sugar levels, giving a continual slow rise and fall rather than the peaks and dips that result from eating processed or sugary foods. Apart from eating complex carbs, there are a number of other things you can do to promote optimal blood sugar balance:

ALWAYS EAT BREAKFAST, as this may help to 'kick start' your metabolism.

NEVER MISS MEALS. Aim to eat three meals a day and two snacks. By eating every two to three hours you will prevent your blood sugar level dropping too dramatically.

BALANCE COMPLEX CARBS with good-quality protein, even when snacking.

AVOID SUGAR and foods containing sugar such as chocolate, sweets, fizzy drinks, alcohol and processed foods. They are rich in quick-releasing sugars, which cause fluctuations in the blood sugar level.

MINIMISE STIMULANTS such as caffeine and cigarettes as these stimulate the body to release its sugar stores, therefore raising the blood sugar level.

DRINK MORE WATER. Dehydration causes fatigue, which can make you crave sugary snacks.

If you follow these tips you will definitely notice a positive difference.

Protein & Essential Fats

Our body is built of proteins. They make up our organs, bones, tendons, ligaments, blood, and our immune system… I could go on. In other words, proteins are key for longevity and recovery. Present in the outer and inner membranes of every living cell, they are vital for a healthy life. Day-to-day wear and tear causes these membranes to break down and so need to be repaired or replaced, making protein a very important part of our diet. If the food we eat is lacking in protein, the body will start digesting its own stores.

Dietary protein is made up of an assortment of 22 different amino acids. Of these, eight are essential – and because our bodies cannot make all of them, we have to get them from food.

Animal sources of protein, such as meat, dairy, fish and eggs, contain all eight essential amino acids and are known as 'first class' or 'complete' proteins. Vegetable sources of protein (with the exception of soya beans) do not contain all eight and are called 'second class' or 'incomplete' proteins. However, this does not mean that a vegetarian diet will be lacking in protein, as the amino acids in one protein can compensate for the deficiencies in another.

Many people struggle to think of a 'protein-rich meal' that doesn't involve either chicken or beef, so the recipes in this book have been carefully chosen to offer varied and less familiar sources of protein such as exotic seafood, game, eggs or soya beans.

Fats are a food group which many of us are reluctant to eat in any quantity. However, not all of them are bad. Essential fats are just that – ESSENTIAL. Our bodies can't make them and so we have to get them from our food. Good sources include raw nuts and seeds, oily fish and soya beans.

As well as being vital for optimal brain function, healthy hair, nails and skin, recent research has shown that essential fats can help beat depression. And they may also help in the control and prevention of a number of diseases including cardiovascular disease, cancers, arthritis and nervous system complaints.

It's a common cooking technique to roast nuts and seeds to bring out the flavour, but actually this decreases their nutritional value – so in all our recipes you will find them used raw and unsalted. To ensure that your diet contains enough essential fats, our three-week plan has been designed to include at least one dietary source every day.

Flavour = Fulfilment

Good-quality, fresh, flavourful and natural ingredients are the basis of what The Pure Package does and we have gone a long way in proving that healthy food can be delicious – our many fans have told us so.

I have always been a great believer in taste and my team understand the importance of tasting everything that leaves our kitchens, from sauces to a single banana or apple. There is just no denying that **flavour = enjoyment = fulfilment**. And by using good-quality ingredients it is much easier to achieve great flavour.

It makes sense to me that foods which have been hidden away in the pantry for weeks or foods that are out of season are not going to deliver on flavour or nutrition. I always do my best to choose **fresh, seasonal, quality ingredients**. Have you ever noticed that a carrot in season has a sweet crunchiness that you just don't get from a carrot grown out of season? And you are much more likely to be satisfied and fulfilled after the fresh, sweet carrot than after the one that tastes of nothing – not to mention the nutritional differences between the two. Similarly, the flavour and nutritional value of a free-range chicken compared to a battery-farmed chicken is huge – and the free-range chicken is good on your conscience too. For me, the difference in flavour is most noticeable when making a stock: free-range bones give a rich, wholesome stock, while the battery-farmed bird gives a stock that is like old dish water!

Now you might find this unbelievable, but **genuine flavour does exist without adding salt**, especially if you use (I know I keep saying it) fresh, quality, ethical and seasonal raw ingredients. You will notice that throughout all of the recipes in this book, there is absolutely no mention of salt. The Pure Package has never compromised on this and never will (it would be much easier to just buy lesser-quality produce and add salt to make it taste of something, but that is not what we are about). It is an unnecessary ingredient that tricks your taste buds and causes water retention. Instead of salt, you will find that we use lots of fresh herbs, spices and great-quality raw ingredients.

WARNING: It does take time for your taste buds to adjust if you have been a salt abuser. Give it a few days and I can assure you, you won't turn back.

In a nutshell, taste is as important as nutrition when it comes to sticking to a healthy diet. You need flavourful dishes in order to feel fulfilled after a meal, and the simplest, most unadulterated way to achieve this is by using quality raw ingredients.

The List

It is a big mistake to underestimate the power of a list. I find that eating ad hoc and on the go makes it very hard to maintain my health goals. Actually, I find that it makes it near impossible. Eating regularly is vital to maintaining a balanced appetite. If you haven't thought about or planned your meals and snacks in advance the chances are that when you are hungry you will grab the nearest thing you can get your hands on, and nine times out of ten it will be something unhealthy – an over-processed sandwich, a chocolate bar, a packet of crisps, a pizza.

For this very reason (as well as to prevent excessive waste), I am a firm believer in using a good old-fashioned shopping list and planning my meals in advance.

I make a grid of Monday through to Sunday, leaving space to plan each of the meals (breakfast, lunch, dinner and snacks) that I intend to have on each day. I focus on making sure each meal contains variety, as well as good sources of carbohydrates (complex ones – see page 18), protein and essential fats (see page 20).

I always check the weather forecast when doing my list as I find the weather affects what I feel like eating.

Planning like this highlights each meal and its ingredients, which I find is key to eating a healthy, balanced, colourful and flavourful diet.

Saying this, when you shop is also important. I have found that the best time for me to food shop is when I am in that happy place of being neither full nor hungry. If I am full, I am just not interested in or inspired by food (whether I have a list or not). If I am hungry, it is disastrous; I pick up all sorts of things that aren't on my list, and can be tempted by food that I would never normally choose to eat.

The illustration shows the grid that I use at home. I hope this helps you as much as it does me. The three-week plan at the back of this book also goes a long way to teaching about food combinations, variety and planning.

STOCKS

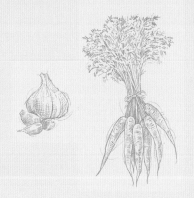

Stocks

MOST RECIPE BOOKS POP A FEW BASIC STOCK RECIPES AT THE END; I am putting them in at the beginning because I want to catch you while you are enthusiastic about following The Pure Package path. Preparing your stocks now will set you up for a flying start as you continue with this book and will really help if you are considering following our three-week healthy eating plan.

I find that home-made stocks always taste better, as stock cubes tend to over-flavour dishes and are particularly salty. Most supermarkets now sell good-quality chicken, beef and duck liquid stocks if you prefer. However, it won't affect the recipes if a stock cube is more convenient to you.

Making vegetable stock is so simple and quick. Once you've tried it, you'll never reach for a stock cube again. It only needs to simmer for 20–25 minutes to extract the maximum flavour from the vegetables.

Vegetable Stock

Makes **1 litre**
Preparation time **10 minutes**
Cooking time **30 minutes**
Wheat free, Gluten free, Dairy free, Vegetarian

INGREDIENTS

1 tablespoon groundnut oil
1 carrot, peeled and roughly chopped
2 onions, peeled and quartered
2 sticks celery, trimmed and roughly chopped
1 leek, trimmed and roughly chopped
3 garlic cloves, left whole and gently bruised
6 black peppercorns
4 flat-leaf parsley stalks
2 bay leaves
1.2 litres water

to serve

PREPARATION

Heat the groundnut oil in a large heavy-based pan over a medium heat. Add the carrot, onions, celery and leek and cook for 3–5 minutes or until beginning to soften. Add the garlic, peppercorns, parsley, bay leaves and pour over the water. Bring to the boil, cover and simmer very gently for 20–25 minutes. Strain through a fine sieve, discard the vegetables and leave to cool.

Use as directed in the recipe within three days or freeze in batches or ice-cube trays for up to three months.

Jennifer's tip Feel free to add whatever vegetables you have to hand to the stockpot. Fennel, tomatoes, mushrooms and broccoli, they all work well.

Chicken Stock

Wherever I am, be it at home, renting a house or on holiday, I always like to have fresh stock to hand, whether it be on the boil or frozen. I make it in huge quantities and freeze in various portion sizes. I don't usually use less than a couple of kilos of chicken bones. You may as well make a huge pot.

Makes **1 litre**
Preparation time **10 minutes**
Cooking time **4 hours**
Wheat free, Gluten free, Dairy free

INGREDIENTS

Free-range chicken bones
2 bulbs garlic, cloves left whole and
gently bruised
water to cover

to serve

PREPARATION

Place the chicken bones and garlic in a large pan and pour over enough cold water to cover. Bring to the boil, skim, then reduce the heat and simmer gently for 3–4 hours, skimming as necessary.

Leave in the refrigerator overnight.

The next day, bring the stock back to the boil and simmer for 1 hour before discarding the bones. Throw the bones away but continue to heat the stock to reduce the liquid.

When the stock is cold it should be jelly-like in consistency with a layer of fat on the top. Remove the fat and use within three days, or freeze for up to three months.

Jennifer's tip Ask your butcher for chicken bones and carcasses when buying other meat. They are often free! I freeze my stock in portions – using my gravy jug as a size guide.

BREAKFASTS

Recipes:

Breakfasts

BREAKFAST IS MY FIRST WAKENING THOUGHT, and without fail gets me up in the morning with a spring in my step. To me it makes perfect sense that my first meal of the day should be something nutritious and delicious, something that will nourish me and set me up for the busy day ahead.

We have all been told countless times by nutritional experts that breakfast is the most important meal of the day, but for many this meal is still a chore. However, not only does a good breakfast give you an energy boost to start the day, it has been linked to many health benefits including weight control and improved mental performance. A healthy, nutritious breakfast reduces hunger throughout the day, allowing us to make better food choices and resist the temptation to succumb to caffeine and sugary treats mid-morning.

The key is not to get stuck in a routine of having the same breakfast every day, but to explore some of the nutritious and delicious options that are out there.

While many of us spend hours daydreaming over what to cook for lunch or dinner, breakfast often gets forgotten, or we take an 'I'll grab something on the way to work' approach. I know that half an hour longer in bed is very tempting, but give yourself that time for breakfast and you are only going to feel the benefits.

A healthy breakfast should always contain good sources of protein and carbohydrate. Protein can come from eggs, yoghurt, nuts, fish or lean meat, and carbohydrate from wholegrains and fruit. It certainly doesn't need to be difficult, and needs to be something delicious you look forward to; I hope I can inspire you.

Home-made muesli is a must for many reasons. Not only can you control what ingredients you use, but you can also make sure your muesli is a good source of essential fats. Most shop-bought muesli is laden with dried fruit and any nuts and seeds are roasted (which destroys their essential fats) – making it high in calories and lacking in nutrients.

Granola Muesli

Makes **40 portions**
Preparation time **10 minutes**
Cooking time **50 minutes**
Wheat free, Vegetarian
Preheat oven to **110°C/Gas ¼**

INGREDIENTS

250ml clear honey
6 sprigs rosemary

250g jumbo porridge oats
250g barley flakes
80g millet flakes
40g maize meal
120g millet grain
40g soya bran

120g pumpkin seeds
120g sunflower seeds
80g linseeds
40g brown rice puffs
80g dried cranberries

to serve
seasonal fresh fruit
natural yoghurt
whole milk (optional)

PREPARATION

Spoon the honey into a small pan. Add the rosemary and warm over a very low heat for 5 minutes to infuse. Remove from the heat and discard the rosemary.

Tip the jumbo oats, barley flakes, millet flakes, maize meal, millet grain and soya bran into a large mixing bowl and mix together. Spread out onto a non-stick baking sheet and drizzle over the honey as evenly as possible. Don't be tempted to mix the honey into the dry ingredients otherwise it will form clumps during cooking. Bake in the oven for 40–50 minutes. Remove from the oven and leave to cool.

Transfer the cooled granola into a large bowl and stir in the pumpkin seeds, sunflower seeds, linseeds, brown rice puffs and dried cranberries. The baked granola will keep in an airtight container for up to one month.

Spoon 120ml yoghurt into a bowl. Add 2 tablespoons of granola and 100–125g seasonal fresh fruit of your choice. If you prefer your muesli runnier, just add some whole milk until it is at the consistency you like.

Jennifer's tip I suggest making a huge batch of this – it is so good for a fast breakfast with yoghurt and fresh fruit and you will find it a number of times in the three-week plan (pages 208–213). If there are any ingredients you can't find, don't worry, simply swap them with other grains you have to hand.

No longer shall porridge have a reputation of being like wallpaper paste. Jazzed up with blackberries it's transformed into a lovely, flavourful breakfast. The protein from the milk combined with the complex carbs in the oats will make you feel fuller for longer.

Apple & Blackberry Porridge

Serves **4**
Preparation time **5 minutes**
Cooking time **10 minutes**
Wheat free, Vegetarian

INGREDIENTS

160g jumbo porridge oats
400ml whole milk
400ml water
3 large apples, cored and cut into bite-size pieces
$\frac{1}{2}$ teaspoon ground cinnamon

100g blackberries

to serve

PREPARATION

Put the porridge oats, milk, water, apple and cinnamon in a non-stick pan over a medium heat. Bring to the boil, reduce the heat and simmer for 4–5 minutes, stirring with a wooden spoon until the oats are tender and creamy.

Stir half of the blackberries through the porridge and remove from the heat.

Spoon the porridge into warmed serving bowls and scatter over the remaining blackberries.

Jennifer's tip It's worth investing in a good heavy-based non-stick pan if you're going to be a regular porridge chef, as washing up anything other than non-stick is tedious with porridge stuck to it.

It's amazing how delicious a small amount of dried prunes can taste, especially when combined with vanilla. For a spicy alternative, soak the prunes overnight with a cinnamon stick and a couple of cloves.

Vanilla, Prune & Pecan Granola Pot

Serves **4**
Preparation time **10 minutes**
Wheat free, Vegetarian

INGREDIENTS

80g ready-to-eat dried prunes, pitted
6 tablespoons water

520ml natural yoghurt
1/4 teaspoon vanilla paste

to serve
120g granola muesli (page 32)
20g pecan nuts, roughly chopped

PREPARATION

Place the prunes in a food processor or blender with the water and blitz to a purée.

In a large bowl, mix the yoghurt and vanilla paste together. Fold through the prune purée to create a marbled effect.

Pour the prune and vanilla yoghurt mix into serving bowls or pots and sprinkle over the granola muesli and roughly chopped pecan nuts.

Jennifer's tip Skin, hair and nails will all benefit from the generous amounts of antioxidant beta-carotene found in prunes. Regular intake of prunes has also been shown to reduce blood cholesterol.

We were trying to come up with something a bit different for breakfast and I always ask my team to give me recipes that really mean something to them. Theresa Ang, one of our team members from Malaysia, mentioned using wild rice and coconut instead of oats and yoghurt. Traditionally called Nasi Satan, this recipe really keeps the taste buds alive.

Wild Rice, Coconut & Mango Bircher

Serves **4**
Preparation time **15 minutes**
Cooking time **20–25 minutes**
Wheat free, Gluten free, Vegetarian

INGREDIENTS	PREPARATION
140g quick-cook wild rice	Cook the rice in a pan of boiling water for 15 minutes or according to packet instructions until tender. Drain.
160ml coconut milk 1 kaffir lime leaf 1 teaspoon clear honey 1 cardamom pod ½ teaspoon vanilla paste 1 star anise	While the rice is cooking, pour the coconut milk into a non-stick pan. Add the lime leaf, honey, cardamom, vanilla and star anise. Bring to the boil, reduce the heat to low and simmer for 10 minutes to allow the flavours to infuse. Pass through a fine sieve and leave to cool. When cool, cover and transfer to the refrigerator.
2 large mangoes, peeled and cubed	Place half of the mango in a food processor and blitz to a purée, or simply mash it with a fork, to save on washing up. Reserve the remaining diced mango.
320ml natural yoghurt	Mix the cooled rice, coconut milk, yoghurt and mango purée together in a large bowl.
small handful coconut flakes	Heat a non-stick frying pan over a medium heat. Add the coconut flakes and dry-fry for 30 seconds, tossing the pan, until golden. Watch carefully as they burn easily. Remove from the heat.
small handful pistachio nuts	Roughly chop the pistachio nuts.
to serve	Spoon the coconut and mango rice into four serving bowls. Top with the diced mango and sprinkle over the toasted coconut and chopped pistachio nuts.

Jennifer's tip This dish is yummy served warm in winter – just mix the ingredients when they are warm instead of letting them cool, or reheat for a couple of minutes in a microwave. Vanilla paste is available in some supermarkets, online and in health food shops and delicatessens. If you can't find it, cut a vanilla pod in half lengthways and scrape out the seeds to use in place of the paste. Instead of discarding the pod, pop it into a storage jar and fill with golden caster sugar to make vanilla sugar.

This brekkie will make you feel like you are visiting the tropics and it is packed with flavour, texture and lots of seedy goodness. Seeds are an excellent nutrition package: they are good sources of protein, among the best plant sources of iron and zinc and they provide more fibre per gram than nuts.

Lime, Banana & Cashew Nut Granola Pot

Serves **4**
Preparation time **10 minutes**
Cooking time **25 minutes**
Wheat free, Vegetarian

INGREDIENTS

80g cashew nuts
6 large bananas, peeled
400ml natural yoghurt
1 teaspoon clear honey
1 tablespoon lime juice, plus extra to taste
grated zest of 1 lime

to serve
120g granola muesli (page 32)
20g pumpkin seeds
20g sunflower seeds

PREPARATION

Place the cashews in a small blender and blitz until broken down. Add the bananas, yoghurt, honey, lime juice and zest to the blender with the cashews and blitz until nice and smooth. Taste and add more lime juice if you fancy a bit more zing.

Pour the banana yoghurt into serving bowls and sprinkle over the granola muesli and seeds.

Jennifer's tip This is really yummy eaten very cold. I used to put it into the freezer if I wanted a healthy, sorbet kind of snack. I recommend making it the night before (it isn't a necessity) but it will go a nice, deep, banana brown and will thicken and intensify in flavour.

Banana & Sultana Bircher Muesli

This breakfast is a real pick-me-up and can be eaten hot or cold — it is naturally sweet and has a slight citrus after-note from the lemon juice.

Serves **4**
Preparation time **10 minutes**
Soaking time **1 hour – overnight**
Wheat free, Vegetarian

INGREDIENTS

3 ripe bananas, peeled and chopped into 1cm pieces
2 tablespoons sultanas
100ml whole milk
400ml natural yoghurt
1½ tablespoons lemon juice
150g jumbo porridge oats

to serve
extra banana pieces
pinch ground cinnamon

PREPARATION

Place the chopped banana and sultanas in a bowl and pour over the milk, yoghurt and lemon juice. Stir in the oats until well combined. Cover and chill in the refrigerator for 1 hour or overnight. You can even make it before you jump in the shower in the morning. By the time you're dressed, it'll be ready to eat.

Give the mixture a good stir. Spoon the muesli into bowls and garnish with banana pieces and cinnamon.

Jennifer's tip You can substitute the bananas with any fruit you fancy — I recommend trying cinnamon-roasted apple, pear or stewed rhubarb and gooseberries.

Bircher muesli is the perfect get-me-up in the morning and is so simple to make. This naturally sweet and delicious recipe can be eaten warm or cold. For those with a sweet tooth, add a drizzle of honey. I never need the honey because I always use very ripe bananas.

Banana & Berry Bircher Muesli

Serves **4**
Preparation time **10 minutes**
Soaking time **1 hour – overnight**
Wheat free, Vegetarian

INGREDIENTS

3 ripe bananas, peeled and chopped into 1cm pieces
100ml whole milk
400ml natural yoghurt
squeeze of lemon juice
150g jumbo porridge oats

to serve
small handful berries per bowl
clear honey, for drizzling (optional)

PREPARATION

Place the chopped banana in a bowl and pour over the milk, yoghurt and lemon juice. Stir in the oats until well combined.

Cover and chill in the refrigerator for 1 hour or overnight. You can even make it before you jump in the shower in the morning. By the time you're dressed, it'll be ready to eat.

Before serving, give the mixture a good stir. Spoon the muesli into serving bowls and sprinkle with the fresh berries. I like blueberries in this dish, but you can use whatever you fancy or what is in season. Drizzle with honey, depending on the ripeness of your banana.

Jennifer's tip If you prefer to eat your muesli warm, simply heat it in a pan over a low heat for 4–5 minutes before adding the berries. This muesli will keep in the refrigerator for up to three days.

Muesli is real fuel for the body and will keep you well stoked all day. It's worth the effort making your own, as shop-bought tends to have a lot of added sugar and this home-made version will keep in the refrigerator for up to three days. Use whatever seasonal fruit you have at home, and in the summer, replace the pears and blackberries with summer berries.

Pear & Blackberry Bircher Muesli

Serves **4**
Preparation time **10 minutes**
Cooking time **10 minutes**
Soaking time **1 hour – overnight**
Wheat free, Vegetarian
Preheat oven to 200°C/Gas 6

INGREDIENTS

4 pears, cored and diced

80g blackberries

160g jumbo porridge oats
100ml whole milk
400ml natural yoghurt

to serve
40g blackberries

PREPARATION

Spread the diced pear in a single layer on a non-stick baking tray. Roast in the oven for 10 minutes until soft. Remove from the oven and leave to cool.

Meanwhile, place the blackberries in a food processor and blitz to a purée. Alternatively, mash with a fork.

Tip the jumbo oats into a large mixing bowl. Add the pear and cooking juices, milk, yoghurt and blackberry purée and mix well together. Leave to soak for 1 hour or overnight.

Spoon into serving bowls and sprinkle with the remaining blackberries.

Jennifer's tip It is important to cook or soak your oats as raw oats contain phytic acid in their outer layer, which can actually block the body's absorption of vital minerals. It will also help to make the oats more digestible.

Strawberry & Mango Bircher Muesli

This is a quick and easy bircher breakfast, but if you have more time or the inclination, purée half the mango flesh and half of the strawberries in a blender first. Fold it through the oat mixture before stirring in the remaining chopped strawberries and mango. Delicious!

Serves **4**
Preparation time **10 minutes**
Soaking time **1 hour – overnight**
Wheat free, Vegetarian

INGREDIENTS

150g jumbo porridge oats
100ml whole milk
400ml natural yoghurt
2 large mangoes, peeled and cubed
140g strawberries, hulled and roughly chopped

to serve
20g sunflower seeds
4 strawberries, hulled and sliced

PREPARATION

Place the oats in a bowl. Pour over the milk and yoghurt. Stir together and add the mango and strawberries, reserving a few cubes of mango to decorate the top if you like. Mix until well combined. Cover and chill in the refrigerator for 1 hour or overnight. You can even make it before you jump in the shower in the morning. By the time you're dressed, it'll be ready to eat.

Give the muesli a good stir and spoon into serving bowls. Sprinkle with sunflower seeds and top with the sliced strawberries and any mango cubes you have reserved.

Jennifer's tip To prepare the mangoes, cut the mango in half down either side of the flat stone that runs through the centre of the fruit, so that you end up with two fleshy halves. Now take each mango half and cut into the flesh, making quite chunky diagonal pieces – take care not to cut through the skin. Turn each half inside out, then slice away the chunks of mango that stand proud from the skin. Cut the flesh from around the stones.

Everybody loves pancakes and I particularly love the smell of them cooking and wafting through the house. A day started with pancakes is a happy day. When you first make these pancakes there is a point just before you add the egg whites where the batter looks like thick gloop; don't panic, it will work.

Oat Pancakes with Fruit & Vanilla Yoghurt

Serves **4**
Preparation time **15 minutes**
Cooking time **25 minutes**
Wheat free, Vegetarian
Preheat oven to 180°C/Gas 4

INGREDIENTS

1 large apple
½ cinnamon stick
1 star anise
3 cloves
pinch grated nutmeg
200ml pomegranate juice
200ml grape juice

20g jumbo porridge oats

240ml natural yoghurt
½ teaspoon vanilla paste

60g jumbo porridge oats
40g brown rice flour
1 teaspoon baking powder
100ml apple juice
½ teaspoon ground cinnamon
2 free-range egg whites, at room temperature
groundnut oil, for oiling

to serve
100g blackberries
60g raspberries
80g blueberries
4 sprigs mint (optional)

PREPARATION

Core the apple, leaving the skin on, and cut into eight segments. Place it in a heavy-based saucepan with the cinnamon stick, star anise, cloves, nutmeg and pomegranate and grape juices and cook over a medium heat for 3 minutes. Remove the apple with a slotted spoon and reserve. Continue to boil the juice and spices for 15 minutes until reduced to a thick syrup, then pass through a fine sieve to remove the spices. Return the syrup to the pan with four of the apple pieces. Cook over a medium heat for 2 minutes. Using a hand-held blender, blitz to a smooth purée. Set aside.

Meanwhile, sprinkle the oats over a non-stick baking sheet and toast in the oven for 5 minutes. Remove from the oven and leave to cool.

In a small bowl, mix the yoghurt and vanilla paste together.

Place the oats, rice flour, baking powder, apple juice and cinnamon in a food processor and blitz to a smooth paste. Transfer to a mixing bowl.

In a clean, grease-free bowl, whisk the egg whites until soft peaks form. Using a large metal spoon, carefully fold the egg whites into the pancake paste, keeping as much air in the mixture as possible.

Heat a large non-stick frying pan over a medium heat. Brush with oil and drop a large tablespoonful of batter per pancake into the pan. This will make pancakes about 6cm across, so you can make four at a time. Cook for about 2 minutes, until small bubbles appear on the surface, then turn and cook for a further 2–3 minutes until golden. Transfer to a warmed plate and cover with kitchen paper while you make another batch. You should have enough batter for eight pancakes.

Either stack the pancakes together on a serving dish or arrange two on each plate. Pour over the pomegranate and apple purée and top with the vanilla yoghurt. Spoon over the reserved poached apple segments and sprinkle the blackberries, raspberries and blueberries around the plate. Scatter over the toasted oats and decorate with the mint, if liked.

Raw Cashew Nut Butter

Raw nut butters are an essential in our house. They're great to have ready made and are so much better for you than shop varieties, which are full of unnecessary ingredients, plus the nuts are often roasted, which converts the essential fats to saturated fats – not good! This is a basic recipe made with cashew nuts, that works equally well with pistachios, peanuts, brazil nuts or almonds. You can store the nut butter for up to a month in the cupboard.

Makes **12 portions**
Preparation time **10 minutes**
Cooking time **25 minutes**
Wheat free, Dairy free, Vegetarian

INGREDIENTS

300g unsalted cashew nuts
6 teaspoons sunflower oil

PREPARATION

Place the cashew nuts in a food processor and blitz on high speed until the nuts are chunky. Add the sunflower oil and continue to blend to a smooth, glossy butter, about 5–10 minutes.

to serve
1 grapefruit per person
rye bread, toasted

Segment one grapefruit per person and spoon the fruit, along with any juice, into a serving bowl. Allow two slices of rye toast per person, spread with 2 tablespoons of nut butter. Cut into triangles and serve with the grapefruit.

Jennifer's tip Making the nut butter is similar to making pastry in a food processor. It starts as a powder, then forms a dough mix and then the oils begin to release from the nuts and it becomes a thick, smooth, glossy butter. Well worth persevering with.

Poached Eggs with Wilted Spinach & Feta Cheese

If there was one food that I could have in abundance it would be eggs. They are a great all-round provider of goodness and are so versatile.

Serves **4**
Preparation time **10 minutes**
Cooking time **10–12 minutes**
Wheat free, Vegetarian

INGREDIENTS

300g baby spinach

1 teaspoon groundnut oil
2 shallots, peeled and finely chopped
30g feta cheese, crumbled
freshly ground black pepper

4 slices rye bread

4 free-range eggs, at room temperature

to serve

PREPARATION

Heat a large pan or wok over a high heat, add the spinach and cook, stirring for 2–3 minutes until wilted. Transfer to a sieve and squeeze to drain.

Return the pan to the heat, add the groundnut oil and shallots and cook over a low heat for 4–5 minutes until soft but not coloured. Return the spinach to the pan, add the feta and cook for 1 minute. Remove from the heat, season with black pepper and set aside.

Bring a pan of water to the boil, ready to poach the eggs.
Toast the rye bread.

While the bread is toasting, crack the eggs gently into the pan. (The water should be just below boiling point, not rapidly boiling.) If you are nervous of poaching, then crack each egg into a cup first and turn them out into the water. Leave to cook for 2–3 minutes until the white is firm and the yolk is soft.

Arrange the rye toast on serving plates, spoon over the spinach and top with the poached eggs. Grind over a little black pepper to taste.

Jennifer's tip To check if your eggs are poached, stick a fork into the white, close to the yolk. It should be firm and not have any stringy, jelly bits attached to the fork when you pull it out. Use the freshest free-range eggs possible for poaching and always have them at room temperature.

When I first started The Pure Package, I would wander round New Covent Garden Market every morning selecting fruit and vegetables for the day. It was here I developed my love of bubble and squeak as it's a breakfast tradition here in the market café.

Bubble & Squeak with Poached Eggs

Serves **4**
Preparation time **15 minutes**
Cooking time **25 minutes**
Wheat free, Gluten free, Dairy free, Vegetarian

INGREDIENTS

300g whole baby potatoes
300g seasonal vegetables, such as leeks, curly kale, cabbage, carrots, broccoli, peas, Brussels sprouts, prepared and finely chopped

2 teaspoons snipped chives
2 teaspoons finely chopped sage
3 spring onions, trimmed and finely sliced
freshly ground black pepper

2 teaspoons groundnut oil

4 free-range eggs, at room temperature

to serve

PREPARATION

Cook the potatoes in a pan of boiling water for 12–15 minutes until tender. Meanwhile, steam the vegetables in a steamer over the pan of potatoes for 7–10 minutes. Drain the potatoes and leave to cool. When the potatoes are cool enough to handle, roughly chop or smash.

Return the potatoes to the pan over a low heat for 1–2 minutes to dry out. Stir in the cooked vegetables, chives, sage and spring onions. Season with black pepper.

Heat the groundnut oil in a large non-stick frying pan. Add the bubble and squeak mixture and press onto the base of the pan. Cook over a medium heat for 4–5 minutes. Flip it over (it doesn't matter if it breaks, as it doesn't have to be in one piece) and cook for a further 4–5 minutes until golden, bubbling and squeaking!

When the bubble and squeak is nearly cooked, poach the eggs. Bring a pan of water to a rolling boil, then reduce the heat so it is just simmering. Crack the eggs gently into the pan (or crack into cups first). Simmer gently for 3 minutes until the white is cooked and the yolk is just beginning to set, but still runny. Remove with a slotted spoon and drain on kitchen paper.

Spoon the bubble and squeak into the centre of four warmed serving plates and lay the poached eggs over the top. Grind over a little black pepper to taste.

Jennifer's tip Bubble and squeak is a dish designed to use up leftovers, so feel free to use whatever vegetables you have in your refrigerator or left over after a big roast.

A delicious, heart-warming bubble and squeak is a great way to start the day, particularly if you've overindulged the night before. I can't resist the sound of it bubbling and squeaking as you fry it up in the pan. Usually I make this with leftover vegetables from the day before, so there is minimal cooking involved, but you can start from scratch and use whatever vegetables are in season.

Bubble & Squeak with Smoked Salmon

Serves **4**
Preparation time **15 minutes**
Cooking time **25 minutes**
Wheat free, Gluten free
Preheat oven to 160°C/Gas 3

INGREDIENTS

300g whole baby potatoes
300g seasonal vegetables, such as leeks, curly kale, cabbage, carrots, broccoli, peas and Brussels sprouts, prepared and finely chopped

2 teaspoons snipped chives
2 teaspoons finely chopped sage
3 spring onions, trimmed and finely sliced
freshly ground black pepper

2 teaspoons groundnut oil

200g smoked salmon

150g cream cheese
2 teaspoons lemon juice
1 teaspoon snipped chives

to serve

PREPARATION

Cook the potatoes in a pan of boiling water for 12–15 minutes until tender. Meanwhile, steam the vegetables in a steamer over the pan of potatoes for 7–10 minutes. Drain the potatoes and leave to cool. When the potatoes are cool enough to handle, roughly chop or smash.

Return the potatoes to the pan over a low heat for 1–2 minutes to dry out. Stir in the cooked vegetables, chives, sage and spring onions. Season with black pepper.

Heat the oil in a large non-stick frying pan. Add the bubble and squeak mixture and press onto the base of the pan. Cook over a medium heat for 4–5 minutes. Flip it over (it doesn't matter if it breaks, as it doesn't have to be in one piece) and cook for a further 4–5 minutes until golden, bubbling and squeaking!

While the bubble and squeak is cooking, line a baking sheet with greaseproof paper. Place the smoked salmon slices on the paper and warm in the oven for 5 minutes.

While the salmon is warming, fold the cream cheese, lemon juice and chives together in a small bowl.

Spoon the bubble and squeak into the centre of four warmed serving plates. Lay the smoked salmon over the top and serve with a dollop of lemon and chive cream cheese.

Cheese Omelette with Grilled Tomato

What could be more simple, but so thoroughly delicious, than a well-cooked omelette? Not undercooked, nor overcooked, with cheese melting through the middle. It's important to learn the basic techniques of omelette making and get confident with it, as from there on in, the variations are endless.

Serves **2**
Preparation time **5 minutes**
Cooking time **8–10 minutes**
Wheat free, Gluten free

INGREDIENTS

2 large tomatoes, halved
freshly ground black pepper

4 free-range eggs, at room temperature
20g Parmesan cheese, finely grated

1 teaspoon groundnut oil
50g mozzarella cheese, torn
50g Cheddar cheese, grated

to serve

PREPARATION

Heat the grill to high. Place the tomatoes on a non-stick baking sheet cut-side down. Season with black pepper and grill for 4 minutes. Turn, season and grill for a further 4–5 minutes.

When the tomatoes are nearly cooked, start cooking the omelette. Heat a large frying pan over a medium heat for 1 minute. Crack the eggs into a bowl and beat them together with the Parmesan. Season with black pepper.

Brush the pan with the groundnut oil. Pour the eggs into the pan. Let the eggs bubble slightly then, using a spatula, draw the mixture in from the sides of the pan a few times, so it gathers in folds in the centre. Leave for a few seconds then stir again to combine the uncooked egg with the cooked. When partly cooked, sprinkle over the mozzarella and Cheddar. Shake the pan a few times over the heat to settle the mixture while it sets. It should look soft to moist on top. Tilt the pan away from you and fold one-third of the omelette over the middle section. Keep the omelette rolling and tip it out onto a large warmed serving platter.

Cut the omelette into pieces and serve with the grilled tomato halves.

Jennifer's tip If you want a fluffier, lighter omelette, separate your eggs and whisk the egg whites to soft peaks, then stir them gently back into the whisked egg yolks. Use a good, flavoursome Cheddar for the best result – my favourite is Montgomery's.

Baby Spinach & Ricotta Omelette

A classic combination that really works. Serve any leftovers with a crisp mixed salad for lunch. It's great for a packed lunch too as it's quite firm, so transports well.

Serves **4**
Preparation time **5 minutes**
Cooking time **15–25 minutes**

Wheat free, Gluten free, Vegetarian
Preheat oven to 200°C/Gas 6

INGREDIENTS

2 large tomatoes, halved
freshly ground black pepper

320g baby spinach
pinch ground nutmeg
100g baby potatoes, cooked and sliced

4 free-range eggs, at room temperature
2 free-range egg whites, at room temperature

1 teaspoon groundnut oil
40g ricotta cheese

to serve

PREPARATION

Place the tomatoes on a baking tray, cut-side up. Season with black pepper and roast in the oven for 10–15 minutes until soft.

While the tomatoes are roasting, wilt the spinach in a saucepan with the nutmeg for 2–3 minutes. Toss together with the potatoes.

Whisk the eggs and egg whites together in a large bowl until light and airy. Season with black pepper.

Preheat the grill to high.

Heat the groundnut oil in an ovenproof non-stick 20cm frying pan over a medium heat. Add the potato and spinach mixture to the pan and pour over the eggs, stirring them for 3–4 minutes until they are half cooked and runny in places. Scatter the ricotta over the omelette and cook under the grill for 3–5 minutes to set the top.

Turn the omelette out onto a chopping board and cut into four or eight wedges. Serve on warmed serving plates with the roasted tomato halves.

Jennifer's tip This is a great way of using up leftover cooked potatoes. Use an electric hand whisk to get plenty of air into the egg mixture.

Cardamom Spiced Kedgeree with Poached Quail's Eggs

A twist on traditional kedgeree, this version is made with quail's eggs and has a delicious Indian influence with the use of cardamom – a perfect brunch for the weekend!

Serves **4**
Preparation time **15 minutes**
Cooking time **25 minutes**
Wheat free, Gluten free

INGREDIENTS

1 tablespoon groundnut oil
1 onion, peeled and finely chopped
pinch ground cardamom
1 teaspoon turmeric
1 cinnamon stick
1 bay leaf

200g brown rice
600ml vegetable stock (page 26), hot
50g hot-smoked mackerel, skinned and flaked
handful flat-leaf parsley, chopped

12–16 quail's eggs

100g watercress, thick stalks removed

to serve
4 dessertspoons (40ml) crème fraîche
1 lemon, cut into quarters

PREPARATION

Heat the groundnut oil in a large saucepan over a medium heat. Add the onion and cook for 3 minutes until soft. Add the cardamom, turmeric, cinnamon stick and bay leaf and cook for a further 1–2 minutes.

Add the rice and stir to coat in the oil and spices. Pour in the hot stock and bring to the boil. Stir once and boil for 5 minutes, then cover the pan and continue cooking the rice on the lowest possible heat for 10 minutes. Add the mackerel and cook for a further 5 minutes or until the rice is cooked. Remove from the heat and stir in the parsley. Keep warm.

Just after you have added the mackerel to the kedgeree pan, bring a small pan of water to simmering point. Crack the quail's eggs and lower them gently into the water. Cook for 2 minutes until softly poached. Remove with a slotted spoon.

While the eggs are poaching, arrange the watercress around the edge of a large serving platter.

Place the mackerel kedgeree in the middle of the serving platter and top with the poached quail's eggs. Put the crème fraîche in a small bowl and place the lemon wedges around the edge of the platter.

Jennifer's tip If you can't get hold of quail's eggs, poach four free-range hen's eggs instead.

LUNCHES

Lunches

LUNCH FOR MOST OF US HAS BECOME LITTLE MORE THAN A PIT STOP. These days, we seem to be always on the go, running from one place to another and lunch seems to have turned into more of a hunger suppresser rather than a meal that you take time out to enjoy. It is now totally acceptable to just grab a sandwich, some crisps and a can of fizz as you dash to that all-important meeting or when you are out with the kids.

In France, however, *tout le monde* takes time out to benefit from a proper lunch – and although I don't always have time to go to the lengths that our European neighbours do, lunch has always been an important meal for me. So much so that I have made the focus of The Pure Package office a huge antique (and coincidentally French) wooden table, where everyone can take time out of their busy day and sit down to enjoy a healthy lunch. Not only is the break important, a healthy balanced lunch can make you more proactive, mentally alert and ready for what the afternoon throws at you.

The recipes in this chapter have been designed to give you the sustenance needed to get you through the day. Nutritionally balanced with the right amount of protein and carbohydrates, you will find that you won't feel stuffed, bloated or low on energy.

You can eat them on the go, at your desk or serve many of them warm when entertaining or eating with the family.

Thai Broth with Prawns & Noodles

Cleansing and comforting, this Thai broth works wonders for me if I'm feeling a little under the weather or just plain tired. If you keep home-made chicken stock in your freezer (see my recipe on page 27) then it takes very little time to make.

Serves **4**
Preparation time **15 minutes**
Cooking time **20 minutes**
Wheat free, Gluten free, Dairy free

INGREDIENTS

1.2 litres chicken stock (page 27)
1 bulb garlic, cloves peeled and crushed
8cm piece fresh ginger, peeled and grated

120g vermicelli rice noodles

350g raw tiger prawns, shelled
1 bunch spring onions, trimmed and finely sliced
100g enoki mushrooms, trimmed
160g mangetout, trimmed and shredded lengthways
120g carrots, peeled and very thinly sliced
160g baby corn, cut into 3 at an angle

to serve
handful coriander, chopped

PREPARATION

Pour the stock into a large pan and bring slowly to the boil. Add the garlic and ginger. Reduce the heat, cover and simmer for 15 minutes.

While the stock is infusing, put the noodles in a heatproof bowl. Cover with boiling water and soak until just tender, about 5 minutes or according to the packet instructions. Drain and rinse under cold water, then drain again.

Add the prawns to the infused stock and cook for 1 minute. Add the spring onions, enoki mushrooms, mangetout, carrots and baby corn. Bring to the boil and remove immediately from the heat, this will only take about 1 minute.

Divide the noodles equally between four warmed serving bowls. Ladle over the hot broth and top with chopped coriander.

Jennifer's tip The vegetables in this broth need to be shredded very thinly as they are added raw and literally cook in the heat of the broth. Use a potato peeler or mandolin to slice the carrots as thinly as you can.

Dramatic in colour and flavour, this soup makes a lovely lunch and is also an excellent canapé served in espresso cups. Friends who proclaim to hate beetroot have tried this and loved it. I like to serve it with hummus toasts for a contrast of flavours and textures.

Lightly Spiced Beetroot & Coconut Soup

Serves **4**
Preparation time **20 minutes**
Cooking time **10 minutes**
Wheat free, Dairy free, Vegetarian

INGREDIENTS

1 teaspoon groundnut oil
1 teaspoon cumin seeds
2 shallots, peeled and finely chopped
2 teaspoons Thai red curry paste
400g peeled cooked beetroot (not in vinegar), roughly chopped

500ml vegetable stock (page 26)
400ml coconut milk
1 tablespoon lime juice

400g can chickpeas, drained
1 tablespoon tahini
pinch ground cumin
1 teaspoon vegetable stock (page 26)
juice of 1/2 lemon

4 slices rye bread
1 tablespoon dessicated coconut (optional)

to serve

PREPARATION

Heat the groundnut oil in a large pan over a medium heat. Add the cumin seeds and cook for 1 minute. When the seeds start crackling, add the shallots and red curry paste and cook over a low heat for 3 minutes or until the shallots are soft. Add the beetroot.

Pour over the vegetable stock and bring to the boil. Reduce the heat and simmer for 2 minutes. Remove from the heat and add the coconut milk and lime juice. Transfer the soup to a blender and blitz until smooth. Return to the pan and warm through, while you make the hummus.

Place the chickpeas, tahini, cumin, vegetable stock and lemon juice in a food processor and blitz to the consistency that you like. You may need to add more stock or some water to loosen the mixture up a little.

Toast the rye bread.

Toast the coconut in a frying pan over a medium heat, taking care not to let it burn.

Spread the hummus over the toasted rye bread and cut into triangles. Ladle the hot soup into four warmed soup bowls, sprinkle with the dessicated coconut, if liked, and serve with the hummus on rye.

Jennifer's tip This soup also freezes well. Freeze in batches for up to three months.

Pea, Feta & Scallop Soup

Scallops have been a favourite of mine since I was a little girl. They were seen as a real luxury and when picking mussels on West Ireland's coast we would sometimes try to catch scallops by hand. I never managed! This soup is visually beautiful and it balances the scallops really well. Try, if you can, to buy hand-dived scallops that are as fresh as possible.

Serves **4**
Preparation time **15 minutes**
Cooking time **25 minutes**
Wheat free

INGREDIENTS

1 teaspoon groundnut oil
½ bunch spring onions, trimmed and finely chopped
1 garlic clove, peeled and finely chopped
500g frozen peas
1 litre vegetable stock (page 26)

large handful basil
1 heaped tablespoon pine nuts
40g feta cheese
dash of olive oil (optional)

4 slices rye bread

8 hand-dived scallops, off the shell, at room temperature
groundnut oil, for brushing

to serve
freshly ground black pepper

PREPARATION

Heat the groundnut oil in a large non-stick saucepan over a low heat. Add the spring onions and garlic and cook for 3–4 minutes until soft but not coloured. Add the peas and vegetable stock. Bring to the boil, cover, reduce the heat and simmer for 18 minutes.

Meanwhile, make the pesto. Place the basil, pine nuts and feta in a food processor and blitz to a smooth paste. Add a dash of olive oil if the mixture is too stiff. Remove half the pesto from the food processor and set aside.

Transfer the soup to the food processor (with half of the pesto still in it). Blitz until smooth. Return the soup to the pan and keep warm over a low heat.

Toast the rye bread. Cut each slice in half and spread with the remaining pesto. Ladle the soup into warmed serving bowls, while you quickly cook the scallops.

Heat a heavy-based frying pan over a high heat. Brush the scallops with groundnut oil, add to the pan and cook for 50 seconds, turn over and cook for a further 50 seconds. Top the soup with the hot scallops.

Grind over some black pepper and serve with the toasted pesto rye bread.

Jennifer's tip When cooking scallops, watch them very carefully, as they literally take seconds to cook. Don't overcook them or they will become rubbery and dry. The beauty is in their salty flavour and succulent texture. They should be soft and slightly translucent when cooked, not hard and white.

Smoked Trout Pâté with Toasted Rye Bread & Carrot Salad

This flavourful lunch takes no time to make and the essential oils in the trout fillets are said to boost brain power.

Serves **4**
Preparation time **10 minutes**
Cooking time **10 minutes**
Wheat free

INGREDIENTS

4 medium carrots, peeled and cut into $1/2$cm slices
$1/4$ teaspoon cumin seeds
$1/2$ teaspoon clear honey
1 teaspoon lemon juice
40g raisins
2 teaspoons olive oil

3 hot-smoked trout fillets, flaked
2 tablespoons crème fraîche
2 teaspoons lemon juice
freshly ground black pepper

8 slices rye bread

small handful coriander, finely chopped

to serve
2 large handfuls lamb's lettuce
20g pine nuts
1 lemon, cut into 4 wedges (optional)

PREPARATION

Steam the carrots over a pan of simmering water for 8 minutes until tender. Drain and transfer to a large bowl. While still warm, add the cumin, honey, lemon juice, raisins and olive oil. Stir to coat in the dressing and leave to cool.

Meanwhile, mix the flaked trout with the crème fraîche and lemon juice in a bowl. Season with black pepper.

Toast the rye bread and cut into triangles.

Stir the finely chopped coriander through the cooled carrot salad.

Spread or pipe the trout pâté onto the rye bread triangles, or serve the pâté in ramekins for people to spread themselves. Arrange the lamb's lettuce on a serving platter. Spoon the carrot salad on top of the leaves. Place the toasts and pâté alongside and sprinkle over the pine nuts. Garnish with a lemon wedge if you like.

Jennifer's tip Resist the urge to toast the pine nuts as, once toasted, the essential fats turn into saturated fats. They still taste yummy untoasted.

Thai Chicken Noodle Salad

Serves **4**
Preparation time **15 minutes**
Cooking time **25 minutes**
Wheat free, Gluten free, Dairy free
Preheat oven to 190°C/Gas 5

While travelling in Thailand, I was lucky enough to study at the Chiang Mai Cookery School. It was there I fell in love with the food and flavours of Thailand. This was and still is one of my favourite recipes.

INGREDIENTS

1 teaspoon tamari soy sauce
1 teaspoon Thai fish sauce
1 teaspoon Thai green curry paste
4 x 80–100g free-range chicken breasts, skin on

1 small red pepper, deseeded
200g mangetout

1 teaspoon tamari soy sauce
1 teaspoon Thai fish sauce
6–8 shiitake mushrooms, thinly sliced

1 small garlic clove, peeled
2cm piece fresh ginger, peeled
2 teaspoons lime juice
1 small red chilli, deseeded
handful coriander
2 teaspoons tamari soy sauce
140ml coconut milk
2 tablespoons water

120g rice noodles

to serve
140g mizuna or baby leaf salad

PREPARATION

In a small bowl, mix the tamari, fish sauce and curry paste together. Rub into the chicken breasts, then place the chicken in a roasting tin and roast in the oven for 25 minutes or until cooked through and tender. Remove from the oven and leave to cool. Discard the skin and slice thinly.

Cut the pepper and mangetout into julienne strips. Set aside.

Heat a wok over a medium heat, add the tamari, fish sauce and mushrooms and stir-fry for 2–3 minutes. Remove from the wok and drain on kitchen paper.

Place the garlic, ginger, lime juice, chilli, coriander, tamari, coconut milk and water in a food processor or blender and blitz to a smooth dressing.

Put the rice noodles in a heatproof bowl. Cover with boiling water and soak until soft, about 10 minutes or according to the packet instructions. Rinse in cold water and drain. Pour half of the dressing over the noodles, reserving the remainder, and toss together.

Combine the mizuna with the other ingredients on a serving platter or in a salad bowl. Drizzle over the remaining dressing and dish out according to the rule of palm (page 15).

Jennifer's tip Rice noodles are most commonly used in the cuisines of Southeast Asia and are available fresh, frozen or dried, in various shapes and thicknesses. Here we use medium-sized dry rice noodles, but feel free to experiment with all types.

Designed by Kevin (who heads up our food development team), this is the most stunning combination of colour, flavour and texture. The freshness of the crisp salad, combined with the soft roasted butternut, spiced couscous, crunchy chickpeas and raspberry vinaigrette is a real winner.

Spiced Butternut & Couscous Salad with Raspberry Vinaigrette

Serves **4**
Preparation time **25 minutes**
Cooking time **25 minutes**
Wheat free, Dairy free, Vegetarian
Preheat oven to 200°C/Gas 6

INGREDIENTS

1 small butternut squash, peeled, deseeded and cut into large dice
3 tablespoons rose harissa

1 teaspoon groundnut oil
1 small red onion, peeled and finely chopped
3 garlic cloves, peeled and crushed
1 teaspoon cumin seeds
1 teaspoon ground coriander
400g can chickpeas, drained
160g barley couscous
320ml vegetable stock (page 26), hot
1 tablespoon finely chopped mint
1 tablespoon finely chopped coriander

50g raspberries
1 tablespoon cider vinegar
2 teaspoons water
1 teaspoon clear honey
1 tablespoon olive oil

½ cucumber
1 pomegranate
200g cherry tomatoes, halved
2 large handfuls baby spinach leaves

to serve
small handful pine nuts

PREPARATION

Tip the squash into a large bowl, add the harissa and toss to coat. Arrange on a non-stick baking tray and roast in the oven for 15–20 minutes until soft.

While the squash is roasting, prepare the couscous. Heat the groundnut oil in a non-stick pan, add the onion and cook for 3–4 minutes until soft but not coloured. Add the garlic, cumin and ground coriander and cook for 2 minutes. Remove from the heat. Add the chickpeas and couscous and pour over the hot stock. Cover with cling film and leave to soak. After 10 minutes, fork through the couscous and stir in the finely chopped mint and coriander.

Place the raspberries, vinegar, water, honey and olive oil in a food processor or blender and blitz to make a dressing. Pour the dressing into a small jug or bowl.

Halve the cucumber lengthways, scoop out the seeds and cut into crescent-shaped pieces. Halve the pomegranate and, using a large spoon, tap the skin to release the kernels. In a large bowl, toss the tomatoes, spinach and cucumber together.

Arrange the spinach salad on a large serving platter. Top with the couscous, scatter over the squash and sprinkle with the pomegranate kernels and pine nuts. Serve with the dressing on the side.

Jennifer's tip Rose harissa is a North African spice paste containing rose petals which are added to balance the fiery heat. It is available in some supermarkets or online.

Salmon & Dill Terrine

This terrine is great for picnics and equally as good as an impressive dinner party starter, all prepared in advance. It's also delicious and just happens to be loaded with healthy, essential fats. Look for organically farmed or wild Alaskan salmon offcuts.

Serves **4**
Preparation time **15 minutes**
Cooking time **10–12 minutes**
Chilling time **4 hours**
Wheat free
Preheat oven to 190°C/Gas 5

INGREDIENTS

300g salmon fillets, skinned

500g baby spinach leaves

small handful of dill, finely chopped
1 tablespoon lemon juice
2 tablespoons crème fraîche
freshly ground black pepper

groundnut oil, for oiling
100g smoked salmon

4 slices rye bread

to serve
160g watercress, thick stalks removed
300g courgettes, trimmed and coarsely grated

PREPARATION

Put the salmon on a non-stick baking sheet and roast in the oven for 10–12 minutes, until cooked. Remove from the oven, leave to cool, then flake into a large bowl, ensuring that any small bones are discarded.

Meanwhile, wilt the spinach in a pan over a medium heat. Squeeze out the excess moisture, then place in a food processor and blitz to a rough purée.

Gently mix the dill, lemon juice, crème fraîche and flaked salmon together to make a light mousse. Season with black pepper.

Lightly oil four small ramekins. Line with cling film, then with the smoked salmon, allowing plenty of overhang. Spoon half of the salmon mousse mixture into the smoked salmon-lined ramekins and press down. Follow with a layer of spinach purée. Spoon the remaining salmon mixture on top of the spinach and fold over the overlapping smoked salmon, then fold over the overlapping cling film to seal in the mixture. Chill in the refrigerator, weighted down, for at least 4 hours but preferably overnight.

Toast the bread when you are ready to eat.

Gently lift the terrines out of the ramekins using the cling film, then remove the film. Place the terrines on serving plates. Arrange the toasted rye triangles, watercress and courgettes around the plate.

Jennifer's tip To weigh down the terrines, place a large handful of baking beans or rice in the centre of a sheet of cling film. Bring the edges of the cling film up together to seal and form a money bag shape. Repeat three more times and place one money bag on top of each ramekin.

I originally came across Gado Gado when travelling in Asia — it is traditionally served from hawkers' carts in Indonesia. Delicately flavoured and with lots of crunch, it is a really satisfying dish.

Gado Gado Salad

Serves **4**
Preparation time **25 minutes**
Cooking time **25 minutes**
Wheat free, Gluten free, Dairy free, Vegetarian

INGREDIENTS

400g baby potatoes, halved
140g fine green beans, trimmed

1 teaspoon groundnut oil
1 teaspoon sesame oil
1 red onion, peeled and finely chopped
1/2 red chilli, deseeded and finely chopped
2cm piece fresh ginger, peeled and finely chopped
250ml coconut milk
4 tablespoons smooth peanut butter (page 49)
2 tablespoons tamari soy sauce
juice of 1/2 lime

4 free-range eggs, at room temperature

50g raw unsalted peanuts
1 tablespoon tamari soy sauce

250g carrots, peeled and cut into julienne strips
1/4 small white cabbage, shredded
1/2 cucumber, cut into julienne strips
120g beansprouts
handful coriander leaves
2 handfuls baby spinach leaves

to serve

PREPARATION

Cook the potatoes in a pan of boiling water for 10 minutes until tender. Drain and leave to cool. Steam the beans over a pan of boiling water for 4–5 minutes.

Meanwhile, make the satay dressing. Heat the groundnut and sesame oils in a pan over a medium heat. Add the onion, chilli and ginger and fry for 4–5 minutes until softened. Stir in the coconut milk, peanut butter, tamari and lime juice. Bring to the boil, reduce the heat and simmer for 10 minutes. Transfer to a food processor or blender and blitz to a smooth dressing. Pour into a jug.

While the dressing is simmering, bring a pan of water to the boil. Add the eggs and cook for 6–7 minutes until hard-boiled. Rinse in cold water until cool enough to handle, peel and cut into thin slices.

While the eggs are boiling, mix the peanuts and tamari together and set aside to marinate.

In a large bowl, mix together the potatoes, carrots, beans, cabbage, cucumber, beansprouts, coriander leaves and spinach until well combined.

Pile the salad onto a large serving plate. Top with the sliced egg and peanuts and drizzle over the satay dressing.

Jennifer's tip Satay sauce is often considered a sin as it's high in fat but you only need a small amount in this dish – plus all the ingredients are good for you... in moderation. Just enjoy it.

Chicken Superfood Salad

This perfectly balanced tangy salad is a great example of clean food packed with flavour. It reminds me of one of our truths — eating the rainbow — using deep purple beetroot with dark green watercress and broccoli: all great tasting and very good for your body.

Serves **4**
Preparation time **15 minutes**
Cooking time **25 minutes**
Wheat free, Dairy free
Preheat oven to 190°C/Gas 5

INGREDIENTS

3 free-range chicken breasts, skin on

60g quinoa, rinsed
120g barley couscous
about 240ml vegetable stock (page 26), hot
1 teaspoon olive oil

500g broccoli, cut into small florets

320g peeled cooked beetroot
½ cucumber

juice of 3 limes
1 tablespoon water

to serve
140g watercress, thick stalks removed
freshly ground black pepper
handful alfalfa sprouts
handful sprouted peas

PREPARATION

Place the chicken breasts on a non-stick baking sheet and roast in the oven for 25 minutes. Leave to cool, discard the skin and cut or shred into thin slices.

Meanwhile, cook the quinoa until just cooked, about 15 minutes or according to the packet instructions. Drain and rinse under cold water. Make the couscous according to the packet instructions, about 4–8 minutes, using vegetable stock and olive oil instead of water.

Steam the broccoli over a pan of simmering water for about 8–10 minutes or until tender.

Cut the beetroot into bite-size pieces. Halve the cucumber lengthways, spoon out the seeds and slice into crescent-shaped pieces.

Whisk together the lime juice and water to make a dressing.

Mix the quinoa, couscous, broccoli, beetroot and cucumber together in a large bowl. Pour over half of the dressing and toss to mix. Use two forks to fold through the dressing and don't overmix or the quinoa and couscous will become lumpy. Be gentle!

Mix the watercress through the quinoa and couscous mixture and season with black pepper. Place in the middle of a large salad bowl or serving platter. Arrange the sliced chicken on top and scatter with alfalfa sprouts and sprouted peas. Serve with the remaining dressing.

Jennifer's tip If you're in a hurry and want a really quick lunch, use bought, ready-cooked roasted chicken and shred the meat from the bone. Serve this salad warm or cook it and chill to serve cold. If serving cold, plunge the broccoli into a bowl of iced water to stop the cooking process.

Gaby, our ops manager, introduced tilapia to our menus — a fish she used to catch with her father on the rivers in Kenya. It is a delicately flavoured white fish that is now more readily available in the UK.

Niçoise Salad

Serves **4**
Preparation time **20 minutes**
Cooking time **20 minutes**
Wheat free, Gluten free
Preheat oven to 200°C/Gas 6

INGREDIENTS

400g baby new potatoes, halved
450g fine green beans, trimmed

8 quail's eggs

4 red peppers, deseeded and cut into julienne strips
4 tilapia fillets, skinned and boned
freshly ground black pepper

60g pine nuts
2 large handfuls basil
1 tablespoon olive oil
40g Parmesan cheese, finely grated

to serve
150g baby spinach leaves
2 tablespoons (60g) pitted black olives
fresh basil leaves, to garnish

PREPARATION

Cook the potatoes in a pan of boiling water for 10 minutes or until almost cooked. Drain and set aside. Meanwhile, steam the green beans for 4–5 minutes or until tender, then drain and plunge into ice-cold water.

While the potatoes are cooking, cook the quail's eggs in a pan of simmering water for 3 minutes until softly boiled. Drain and cover in cold water. When cool enough to handle, shell and cut in half.

Place the peppers on a non-stick roasting tray and roast in the oven for 15 minutes. Season the tilapia fillets with black pepper and add them to the roasting tray for the final 8 minutes of the cooking time. Remove from the oven when the fish is just cooked and the peppers are soft.

While the fish is cooking, make the pesto. Place the pine nuts, basil, olive oil and Parmesan in a food processor and blitz to a purée.

Make a bed of spinach in a large serving bowl. Place the potatoes and green beans in the middle. Top with the fish and scatter the red pepper over. Drizzle the pesto over the salad and scatter the olives and quail's eggs around the bowl. Sprinkle over the basil leaves.

Jennifer's tip Once upon a time, I would have used seared tuna in this dish, but due to overfishing I feel much more comfortable with an alternative. If you can't find tilapia easily, use sea bream or sea bass instead.

Roasted Vegetable & Feta Salad

I am a huge fan of cheese – I like to think of it as being part of my DNA (having grown up on a cheese farm in Ireland) and I love this salad – the saltiness of the feta and olives goes perfectly with the roasted vegetables.

Serves **4**
Preparation time **20 minutes**
Cooking time **20 minutes**
Wheat free, Gluten free, Vegetarian
Preheat oven to 200°C/Gas 6

INGREDIENTS

4 medium courgettes, trimmed
1 small butternut squash, deseeded

400g fine green beans, trimmed

8 sprigs thyme, leaves only

5 tablespoons balsamic vinegar
2–3 tablespoons water

to serve
100g baby spinach leaves
200g feta cheese, crumbled
1/2 jar (140g) sun-dried tomatoes in oil, drained
small handful basil, leaves only
100g pitted black olives

PREPARATION

Cut the courgette and squash into bite-size pieces and tip into a non-stick roasting tray. Roast in the oven for 15–20 minutes, shaking halfway through cooking.

Meanwhile, steam the beans for 4–5 minutes. Drain and plunge into ice-cold water. This helps to stop them overcooking, keeping the nutrients in and the natural bright green colour.

When you take the vegetables out of the oven, mix through the thyme leaves.

Whisk the vinegar and water together in a small bowl to make a dressing. Decant into a serving jug.

Use the spinach leaves to form a base in your salad bowl, and layer on the beans and thyme-roasted vegetables. Top with the feta, sun-dried tomatoes, basil and olives. Serve with the dressing on the side.

Jennifer's tip There's no need to add oil to vegetables when roasting, a non-stick tray is all you will need.

Warm Teriyaki Chicken Salad

Serves 4
Preparation time 15 minutes
Marinating time 1 hour – overnight
Cooking time 25–30 minutes
Wheat free, Gluten free, Dairy free
Preheat oven to 190°C/Gas 5

It's surprisingly easy to make your own teriyaki sauce and after you've made it once you won't buy ready-made again. This salad can be served warm or cold and is delicious not only with chicken, but salmon too.

INGREDIENTS

3 tablespoons cider vinegar
6 tablespoons tamari soy sauce
3 tablespoons mirin
1 tablespoon clear honey
1 garlic clove, peeled and crushed
1 teaspoon ground ginger

3 free-range chicken breasts, skin on
150g shiitake mushrooms, thinly sliced

220g brown rice
1 tablespoon black sesame seeds
400g tenderstem broccoli florets

140g beansprouts
120g red chard, torn into pieces
100g radicchio, torn into pieces
1 tablespoon black sesame seeds

to serve

PREPARATION

To make the teriyaki marinade/dressing, pour the vinegar into a small pan with the tamari, mirin and honey. Add the garlic and ginger and heat over a low heat until the honey has dissolved. Remove from the heat and set aside to cool.

Marinate the chicken and mushrooms (separately) in a quarter of the marinade/dressing in shallow dishes. Cover and chill in the refrigerator for 1 hour or overnight.

Once you are ready to start cooking, bring a large pan of water to the boil for the rice. Place the chicken breasts skin-side up on a non-stick baking sheet and roast in the oven for 25 minutes, until cooked.

Add the rice to the pan and cook for 20–25 minutes or according to the packet instructions, until tender. Drain, return to the pan and pour another quarter of the marinade/dressing into the cooked rice. Add the sesame seeds and stir.

After the rice has been cooking for 15 minutes, set the broccoli over a pan of simmering water to steam for 8 minutes or until tender. Lightly sauté the mushrooms (with their marinade) over a medium heat until soft.

Remove the chicken from the oven, discard the skin and cut the meat into strips. Pour another quarter of the marinade/dressing into a small bowl and add the chicken. Toss to coat.

In a large bowl, mix together the sautéed mushrooms, steamed broccoli, beansprouts, red chard, radicchio and the remaining quarter of the marinade/dressing until well combined.

Spoon the rice around the edge of a serving platter and place the chicken and vegetables in the centre. Serve family style on the table and dish according to the rule of palm (page 15).

Sweet Potato, Beetroot & Tymsboro Goat's Cheese Salad

You will be eating the rainbow with this salad – a classic combination of beetroot, sweet potato and goat's cheese… with the added surprise of tarragon, which complements and counteracts the other ingredients' sweetness.

Serves **4**
Preparation time **10 minutes**
Cooking time **30 minutes**
Wheat free, Gluten free
Preheat oven to 200°C/Gas 6

INGREDIENTS

600g sweet potatoes, cut into 2.5cm chunks
2 teaspoons black sesame seeds

400g peeled cooked beetroot, cut into large dice
1 teaspoon balsamic vinegar

1 tablespoon balsamic vinegar
1 tablespoon water

4 handfuls watercress, thick stalks removed
240g sugar snap peas
2 tablespoons finely chopped tarragon
freshly ground black pepper

to serve
140g Tymsboro goat's cheese, crumbled or cut into bite-size pieces

PREPARATION

Tip the sweet potatoes into a non-stick roasting tin and roast in the oven for 30 minutes or until soft. Remove from the oven and, when cool enough to handle, toss together with the sesame seeds.

In a mixing bowl, mix the beetroot and vinegar together and set aside.

Whisk the vinegar and water together to make a dressing.

In a large mixing bowl, mix together the watercress, sugar snap peas, tarragon and half of the dressing until well combined. Season with black pepper.

Arrange the watercress salad on a large serving platter. Top with the roasted sesame sweet potato, beetroot and crumbled goat's cheese. Drizzle over the remaining dressing.

Jennifer's tip If you can't find Tymsboro, or would like to make this dish vegetarian, any other goat's cheese can be substituted – but remember that the better the cheese you buy, the yummier your salad.

Asparagus & Feta Frittata

This is one of those all-round dishes that is perfect for breakfast, lunch, dinner or picnics.

Serves **4**
Preparation time **10 minutes**
Cooking time **10 minutes**
Wheat free, Gluten free, Vegetarian

INGREDIENTS

400g asparagus tips, trimmed
2 teaspoons groundnut oil
200g new potatoes, cooked and sliced

2 teaspoons red wine vinegar
2 teaspoons olive oil
freshly ground black pepper
2 plum tomatoes, roughly chopped
1 shallot, peeled and
finely chopped

6 free-range eggs, at room
temperature
80g feta cheese, crumbled
small bunch chives, snipped

2 teaspoons groundnut oil

to serve
2 handfuls mixed salad leaves

PREPARATION

Remove the woody ends of the asparagus by bending them and snapping where they break naturally. Discard the woody stalk and cut the remaining stem into pea-sized pieces.

Heat the groundnut oil in a pan. Add the potatoes and cook for 3 minutes, then add the asparagus and cook for a further 2 minutes. Remove from the heat and set aside.

Whisk the vinegar and olive oil together in a large bowl to make a dressing. Season with black pepper. Add the tomatoes and shallot and set aside while you cook the frittata.

Break the eggs into a bowl, add the feta and beat lightly together. Stir in the chives and season with black pepper.

Preheat the grill to high. Heat the groundnut oil in a 20cm ovenproof frying pan. Add the egg mixture and cook for 2 minutes, stirring gently. Stir in the potatoes and asparagus and cook over a low heat, loosening the egg from the side until just setting (it should still be quite runny). When the base is golden, pop the frying pan under the grill and cook for 2–3 minutes until set.

Loosen the frittata from the pan with a fish slice and flip it over onto a chopping board. Cut into wedges and serve with the dressed tomatoes and mixed leaf salad.

Jennifer's tip To make this frittata fit with the seasons, substitute the asparagus with peas, broad beans or edamame beans instead.

Smoked Venison Salad

I think pears are vastly underused and work just as well in savoury dishes as they do in desserts. They absorb flavours really well and make a great accompaniment to cold meats.

Serves **4**
Preparation time **10 minutes**
Cooking time **20–25 minutes**
Wheat free, Gluten free

INGREDIENTS

120ml apple juice
120ml water
3 large pears, cored and cut into thin wedges
80ml balsamic vinegar

400g asparagus tips, trimmed

2 large handfuls rocket

to serve
200g smoked venison, thinly sliced
20g Parmesan cheese, shaved
60g walnuts
freshly ground black pepper

PREPARATION

Bring the apple juice and water to the boil in a pan. Add the pears and poach over a low heat for 12–15 minutes until tender. Remove the pears with a slotted spoon and drain on kitchen paper. Return the pan to the heat. Add the vinegar, bring to the boil, lower the heat and simmer until reduced by half. Remove from the heat and leave to cool.

Bring a pan of water to the boil. Add the asparagus and cook for 2–3 minutes until tender. Drain.

In a large mixing bowl, mix the rocket, asparagus and balsamic vinegar reduction until well combined.

Arrange the rocket salad on one large platter and scatter over the pears, venison slices, Parmesan and walnuts. Season with black pepper. Dish individually according to the rule of palm (page 15).

Jennifer's tip You can buy smoked venison at some supermarkets, otherwise order it online from The Pure Package's supplier Upton Smokery (www.uptonsmokery.co.uk).

Chef Ulrika designed this dish last winter – it is a great twist on the classic risotto and spelt is a healthy alternative to Arborio rice. If you're not familiar with spelt don't be discouraged, it's a much underused grain that has a lovely bite and absorbs flavours really well. If you can't find pearl spelt, substitute with pearl barley.

Spiced Pearl Spelt, Goat's Cheese & Walnut Salad

Serves **4**
Preparation time **20 minutes**
Cooking time **25 minutes**
Wheat free
Preheat oven to **200°C/Gas 6**

INGREDIENTS

1 teaspoon groundnut oil
1 teaspoon cayenne pepper
1 teaspoon ground cumin
1 teaspoon dried oregano
1 small butternut squash, peeled, deseeded and cubed

1 teaspoon groundnut oil
1 small red onion, peeled and finely chopped
1 teaspoon turmeric
160g pearl spelt
350ml vegetable stock (page 26), hot

40g walnut halves
1 tablespoon chopped basil

40g sun-dried tomatoes in oil, drained
3 tablespoons balsamic vinegar
about 3 tablespoons water
pinch dried chilli flakes

400g peeled cooked beetroot
120g baby spinach leaves

to serve
120g Ragstone goat's cheese log

PREPARATION

Mix the groundnut oil, cayenne, cumin and oregano together in a large bowl. Add the butternut squash cubes and toss to coat in the spice paste. Use your fingers to rub the spices into the squash.

Spread the squash out in a single layer in a non-stick ovenproof dish and roast in the oven for 15–20 minutes or until soft. Remove from the oven and set aside.

Meanwhile, heat the oil in a large, heavy-based pan. Add the onion and cook over a low heat for 3–4 minutes until soft but not coloured. Add the turmeric and spelt and stir to coat the spelt in the spice and oil.

Pour in a quarter of the stock and simmer over a medium heat, stirring. Once the liquid has been absorbed, add more stock a little at a time and continue to simmer and stir until all the liquid has been absorbed, about 20 minutes. The creamy texture of a good risotto is a result of slow cooking and constant stirring, so don't be tempted to add all the liquid at once. If the stock runs out before the spelt is cooked, add a splash of hot water. Remove from the heat.

Roughly chop half the walnuts, leaving the remainder whole. Stir the chopped nuts and basil into the spelt once it is cooked, reserving the whole nuts.

Place the sun-dried tomatoes, vinegar, water and chilli flakes in a food processor or blender and blitz to a smooth dressing. If you want the dressing slightly runnier, add a little more water until the consistency is right for you.

Cut the beetroot into bite-size pieces, tip into a large bowl and add the spinach leaves. Pour over the dressing and toss together.

Arrange the spinach and beetroot around the edge of a salad bowl or platter. Spoon the warm spelt into the middle and top with the squash. Crumble the goat's cheese over the top and scatter with the whole walnut pieces. Serve family style on the table and dish according to the rule of palm (page 15).

Jennifer's tip If you would like to make this dish vegetarian simply replace the Ragstone with a vegetarian goat's cheese.

Goat's Cheese, Sun-dried Tomato & Lamb's Lettuce Salad

This classic combination works every time and never ceases to please. So many people have asked me for the dressing recipe, which makes me smile as it's simply a mixture of balsamic vinegar and water.

Serves **4**
Preparation time **20 minutes**
Cooking time **25 minutes**
Wheat free, Gluten free, Vegetarian
Preheat oven to 200°C/Gas 6

INGREDIENTS

2 yellow peppers, deseeded and cut into bite-size pieces

360g baby new potatoes

2 tablespoons water
2 tablespoons balsamic vinegar

1 small cucumber
160g lamb's lettuce or baby spinach leaves

to serve
200g sun-dried tomatoes in oil, drained
20g pine nuts
120g Golden Cross goat's cheese, cut into 4 rounds
edible flowers, to garnish (optional)

PREPARATION

Spread the pepper pieces in a single layer in a non-stick ovenproof dish. Roast in the oven for 15–20 minutes until the peppers are soft. Remove from the oven and leave to cool.

Meanwhile, cook the potatoes in a pan of boiling water for 10–12 minutes until tender. Drain and, when cool enough to handle, slice each potato into three pieces.

While the potatoes are cooking, mix the water and vinegar together to make a dressing. Pour into a small jug or bowl and set aside.

Halve the cucumber lengthways, scoop out the seeds and slice into crescent-shaped pieces. Place the lamb's lettuce, cucumber, sliced warm potatoes and roasted peppers in a large bowl and toss together.

Preheat the grill to high.

Spoon the salad into a large serving bowl. Top with the sun-dried tomatoes and sprinkle over the pine nuts.

Place the goat's cheese rounds on a non-stick baking sheet and grill for 1 minute until golden and beginning to melt. Remove from the grill and place on top of the salad. Sprinkle with the flowers, if using, and serve with the dressing on the side.

Jennifer's tip Eating potatoes with their skin on increases their fibre content, which in turn helps to slow down the release of the carbohydrate's sugar into the bloodstream.

Wasabi Brown Rice & Soya Bean Salad

Serves **4**
Preparation time **20 minutes**
Cooking time **20–25 minutes**
Wheat free, Gluten free, Dairy free, Vegetarian
Preheat oven to 200°C/Gas 6

I am nothing if not overexcited about the virtues of the soya bean. It's pure genius. Not only is it instantly convenient, it's also an incredible source of protein and has a lovely bite. This salad is packed with flavour and is really simple to make.

INGREDIENTS

¹⁄₂ small butternut squash, deseeded and cut into bite-size pieces

100g brown rice
1 bouquet garni

200g asparagus tips, trimmed
300g frozen soya beans, defrosted

2 handfuls rocket
4cm piece cucumber
4 tablespoons brown rice vinegar
3 tablespoons olive oil
1 tablespoon wasabi paste
small handful coriander

¹⁄₂ bunch spring onions, trimmed and finely chopped
small handful flat-leaf parsley, finely chopped

1 pomegranate

to serve
100g rocket

PREPARATION

Tip the squash onto a non-stick roasting tray and roast in the oven for 15–20 minutes. Remove from the oven and leave to cool.

Meanwhile, cook the rice in a pan of boiling water with the bouquet garni for 20–25 minutes or according to the packet instructions until tender. Drain, then tip into a large bowl and discard the bouquet garni. Set aside.

Bring a saucepan of water to the boil, add the asparagus and cook for 1 minute. Add the soya beans and cook for a further minute. Drain and cool under cold water. Pat dry and add the soya beans and asparagus to the bowl with the rice.

Place the rocket, cucumber, vinegar, olive oil, wasabi paste and coriander into a food processor or blender and blitz to a smooth green dressing. You may want to add some water to get it to the consistency you like.

Mix the finely chopped spring onions and parsley through the rice.

Halve the pomegranate and, using a large spoon, tap the skin of the fruit to release the kernels.

Arrange the rocket on four serving plates. Spoon over the rice, soya bean and asparagus mixture and top with the roasted squash. Pour over the dressing and garnish with the pomegranate kernels.

Jennifer's tip Wasabi, most commonly used as an accompaniment for sushi, is a fiery horseradish so a little goes a long way. Don't overdo it in this recipe or it will overpower the dressing.

Feta & Herb Lentil Salad

Herbs are packed with goodness and flavour, and their intensity of smell and flavour reflect just how good they are for you. The more pungent the better.

Serves **4**
Preparation time **20 minutes**
Cooking time **20 minutes**
Wheat free, Gluten free, Vegetarian

INGREDIENTS

200g Puy lentils

240g fine green beans, trimmed

1 tablespoon chopped flat-leaf parsley
1 tablespoon snipped chives
1 sprig thyme, leaves only
1 tablespoon chopped mint
1 tablespoon olive oil
juice of 1 lemon
3 tablespoons balsamic vinegar

3 carrots, peeled
3 sticks celery, trimmed

to serve
120g baby spinach leaves
240g feta cheese

PREPARATION

Cook the lentils in a pan of boiling water for 15–20 minutes or until tender. Drain.

Meanwhile, cook the beans in a pan of boiling water for 4–5 minutes until tender. Drain and plunge into ice-cold water.

Place the lentils in a large bowl. Add the parsley, chives, thyme, mint, olive oil, lemon juice and vinegar and toss together until well combined.

Cut the carrots and celery into julienne strips and fold into the dressed lentils.

Arrange the baby spinach on a large serving platter. Scatter the fine green beans over the spinach and spoon over the lentil salad. Crumble the feta cheese over the top.

Jennifer's tip To prepare blanched vegetables for salads, have a large bowl of water, filled with ice, at the ready. As soon as you take the vegetables off the heat, drain and plunge them into the ice-cold water. Lift out with a slotted spoon and drain on kitchen paper to dry them off. Once dry, any dressings will stick to them, rather than slip off, as happens if they're still wet.

Crab, Chilli & Rocket Salad

Growing up in the west of Ireland, fresh crab was something that was often served at the family table and I remember fighting with my siblings to get the claws! This salad is great for a quick lunch during lazy summer days.

Serves **4**
Preparation time **20 minutes**
Cooking time **5 minutes**
Wheat free, Gluten free, Dairy free

INGREDIENTS

120g vermicelli rice noodles

1 teaspoon sesame oil
1 red chilli, deseeded and finely chopped
1 lemongrass stalk, finely chopped
1cm piece fresh ginger, peeled and finely chopped
1 tablespoon mirin

350g white crabmeat
1 red chilli, deseeded and finely chopped
large handful coriander, finely chopped
grated zest of 1 lime

3cm piece fresh ginger, peeled
1 red chilli, deseeded
small handful coriander
3 tablespoons tamari soy sauce
1 tablespoon sesame oil
2 tablespoons water

200g mangetout, trimmed
200g red cabbage

to serve
180g rocket
1 lime, cut into 4 wedges

PREPARATION

Put the noodles in a heatproof bowl and cover with boiling water. Leave to soak until just tender, about 5 minutes or according to the packet instructions. Drain and rinse under cold water, then drain again.

Heat the sesame oil in a small frying pan. Add the chilli, lemongrass and ginger and cook for 1 minute. Add the mirin, remove from the heat and toss through the noodles. Cover and set aside to allow the flavours to develop.

Mix the crabmeat with the chilli, coriander and lime zest.

To make the dressing, place the ginger, chilli, coriander, tamari, sesame oil and water in a small food processor or blender and blitz to a paste.

Decant into a serving jug.

Cut the mangetout into julienne strips. Using a mandolin or sharp knife, slice the red cabbage very (paper) thin.

Arrange the rocket, noodles, red cabbage, mangetout and crab mixture on a serving plate. Garnish with a lime wedge and serve the dressing on the side.

Jennifer's tip For a special meal I like to garnish this dish with baby crab claws in the shell. Ask your fishmonger if he can get hold of them for you.

Puy Lentil
& Salmon Salad

A great combination, Puy lentils work particularly well with oily fish. In this recipe the warm lentils are given a cheeky tang with a herb, chilli and mustard dressing and then topped with the steamed salmon straight from the oven. If you're cooking this for friends, serve the salmon in the foil parcels and let your guests open them at the table and experience the mouthwatering aroma for themselves.

Serves **4**
Preparation time **15 minutes**
Cooking time **20 minutes**
Wheat free, Gluten free, Dairy free
Preheat oven to 200°C/Gas 6

INGREDIENTS	PREPARATION
3 red peppers	Halve and deseed the peppers and cut them into 5mm dice. Spread the peppers out on a non-stick baking sheet and roast in the oven for 10 minutes until soft. Remove from the oven, set aside, and turn the oven down to 180°C/Gas 4.
3 sticks celery, trimmed **2–3 handfuls cherry tomatoes**	Finely chop the celery and halve the cherry tomatoes.
160g Puy lentils	Cook the lentils in a pan of boiling water for 15–20 minutes or until just tender.
2 tablespoons chopped parsley **2 tablespoons chopped dill** **2 teaspoons Dijon mustard** **½ small green chilli, deseeded** **4 tablespoons lemon juice** **2 teaspoons olive oil**	Meanwhile, make the dressing. Place the parsley, dill, mustard, chilli, lemon juice and olive oil in a food processor and blitz until smooth. If necessary, add a dash of water to get the right consistency.
1 tablespoon chopped dill	Drain the lentils, tip into a bowl while still warm and toss with half of the dressing (reserve the remaining dressing), the diced roasted peppers, chopped celery, halved tomatoes and chopped dill. Cover and set aside.
4 x 80–100g salmon fillets, skinned **4 tablespoons white wine**	Cut four 20cm squares of foil. Place one salmon fillet in the middle of each sheet. Gather up the edges to form a parcel. Pour a tablespoon of wine over each piece of salmon and seal the parcel so it is airtight. Place the foil parcels on a baking sheet and roast in the oven for 10 minutes or until the salmon is just cooked through.
to serve **120g lamb's lettuce** **1 lemon, cut into 4 wedges (optional)**	Arrange some lamb's lettuce on a serving plate. Spoon the lentil mix into the middle and top with a portion of hot salmon. Garnish with a lemon wedge if you like and serve with the remaining dressing on the side.

There is absolutely no denying this is simply one of the tastiest lunches around. It can either be eaten warm or alternatively it is delicious cold, when cooked in advance. And as salmon is bursting with essential fats, it is very good for you too.

Sesame Salmon & Rice Noodle Salad

Serves **4**
Preparation time **15 minutes**
Cooking time **10–12 minutes**
Wheat free, Gluten free, Dairy free
Preheat oven to 180°C/Gas 4

INGREDIENTS

4 x 80–100g salmon fillets, skinned

2 grapefruits
2 red peppers, deseeded
100g mangetout, trimmed

120g rice noodles

handful salad leaves
2 teaspoons sesame oil

2 tablespoons black sesame seeds
20 mint leaves
20 coriander leaves

to serve
2 tablespoons tamari soy sauce
2 tablespoons mirin

PREPARATION

Line a baking tray with baking parchment or use a non-stick tray. Place the salmon fillets onto the tray. Place on the middle shelf of the oven and cook for 10–12 minutes or until just cooked.

While the salmon is cooking, peel the grapefruits and cut into segments. Thinly slice the red peppers and mangetout into strips.

Empty the rice noodles into a large heatproof bowl. Boil the kettle and pour enough hot water over the noodles to cover them. Stir and leave to stand for 6–8 minutes or according to the packet instructions until just soft. Drain through a colander. If you are making this in advance you can put the noodles straight into cold water to stop the cooking process and keep them fresh.

Arrange the salad leaves on serving plates. Mix the drained noodles with the sesame oil and place in the centre of the salad.

Remove the salmon fillets from the oven and immediately sprinkle with black sesame seeds. Place the sesame salmon on top of the noodles and scatter the mangetout and red pepper strips, grapefruit segments, mint and coriander around the dish.

Mix the tamari and mirin together in a jug and pour over the salad to taste.

Jennifer's tip Grapefruit segments are delicious added to all kinds of salads. We find the best way to get clean segments is to cut a thin slice off the top and bottom of the grapefruit to create a flat surface. Then glide your knife down the sides of the grapefruit, following the contour to remove the peel and pith. Discard any peel or skin. Make a small cut with your knife following the inside membrane of a segment, cut down the other side until the slice meets in the middle and your perfectly prepared segment should pop out. Continue until you have prepared all segments of the grapefruit.

Chicken with Coconut Noodles & Asian Coleslaw

A delicious combination of coconut-infused chicken with noodles and crunchy Asian coleslaw. It's worth the time and effort infusing the coconut milk and leaving it to cool, but if you don't have time or patience, serve it warm.

Serves **4**
Preparation time **25 minutes**
Cooking time **20 minutes**
Wheat free, Gluten free, Dairy free

INGREDIENTS

250ml coconut milk
3 tablespoons lime juice
2 kaffir lime leaves
$1/2$ red chilli, deseeded and finely chopped

1 teaspoon groundnut oil
300g free-range chicken breast, cut into bite-size pieces

140g rice noodles
small handful coriander, finely chopped

3 tablespoons lime juice
4 tablespoons balsamic vinegar
1 tablespoon Thai fish sauce
$1/2$ red chilli, deseeded and finely chopped

300g baby carrots, halved
$1/4$ small white cabbage, shredded
$1/4$ small red cabbage, shredded

to serve
handful mint leaves

PREPARATION

First make the dressing by pouring the coconut milk into a small pan. Add the lime juice, lime leaves and chilli. Heat over a low heat to near boiling. Remove from the heat and leave to cool to allow the flavours to infuse. Discard the lime leaves before serving.

Heat the groundnut oil in a non-stick frying pan. Add the chicken and stir-fry for 4–5 minutes until cooked. Remove from the heat and transfer to a bowl. Pour over half of the coconut dressing and set aside.

Put the rice noodles in a heatproof bowl and cover with boiling water. Leave to soak until soft, about 10 minutes or according to the packet instructions. Drain and return to the bowl. Pour over the remaining coconut dressing and stir in the coriander. Set aside.

While the chicken and noodles are cooling, make the coleslaw. Whisk the lime juice, vinegar, fish sauce and chilli together to make a dressing.

In a large mixing bowl, mix the carrot and white and red cabbage with the dressing until well combined. Set aside.

Place the coleslaw on a serving platter, and scatter over the mint leaves. Top with the coconut noodles and finally the chicken.

Jennifer's tip The coleslaw is a great all-round recipe which works with other fish and meats, especially as an accompaniment to a barbecue.

DINNERS

Recipes:

Dinners

THE RECIPES IN THIS CHAPTER ARE HOMELY DINNERS FOR YOU TO ENJOY with both friends and family. In my house, dinner is a time to reconnect as a unit after a busy day. What we eat needs to be both comforting and nourishing, using recipes that are easy to make – I love involving my children in the preparation of parts of the recipes as a way to teach them more about food and where it comes from.

I have probably inherited this from my father – he was always (and still is!) in charge of cooking the family dinner – it was the highlight of the day – so much so that he and I would chat and plan it as soon as I was downstairs for breakfast each morning. Even now, despite living in a different country, our phone conversations always start with me asking him what his plan is for dinner! I am sure when my kids are old enough they will be asking me 'what's for dinner?' at breakfast time – and I can't wait.

I find that meals are always more tricky if you do not plan for them. Growing up on a small cheese farm taught me how vital thinking ahead is when it comes to food – and a good dinner. I remember my dad cooking roast beef and at the last minute we realised we had forgotten the horseradish, and there is nothing romantic about searching and hurrying around in the dark to dig up the potent root, I can tell you.

So, with all this in mind, take the time to plan what you are going to eat for dinner, and don't eat too late. I hope you get as much pleasure out of cooking and eating these comforting recipes as I do, and remember, as with breakfast and lunch, your dinner should combine a good balance of protein and carbohydrates.

Chicken & Noodle Laksa

This laksa recipe was devised by Gaby, our ops manager, on her return from holidaying in Singapore. Laksa is a spicy layered noodle soup that's incredibly comforting. It's really warming in the winter, but also light and aromatic for breezy summer evenings.

Serves **4**
Preparation time **35 minutes**
Cooking time **20 minutes**
Wheat free, Gluten free, Dairy free

INGREDIENTS

½ red chilli, deseeded
2 lemongrass stalks, roughly chopped
4 garlic cloves, peeled
3cm piece fresh ginger, peeled and roughly chopped

1 teaspoon groundnut oil
½ onion, peeled and finely chopped
320g free-range chicken breast, cut into bite-size pieces

400ml coconut milk
2 kaffir lime leaves
400ml vegetable stock (page 26), hot

240g pad Thai rice noodles

2 teaspoons Thai fish sauce
1 red pepper, deseeded and cut into julienne strips
120g beansprouts
100g sugar snap peas, cut into julienne strips
½ spring onion, trimmed and cut into julienne strips

to serve
small handful coriander, leaves only
35g raw unsalted cashew nuts, roughly chopped

PREPARATION

Place the chilli, lemongrass, garlic and ginger in a small food processor and blitz to a paste.

Heat the groundnut oil in a wok or large non-stick frying pan. Add the paste and chopped onion and cook, stirring, for 4–5 minutes until the onion begins to soften. Add the chicken and cook for a further 5 minutes.

Add the coconut milk, lime leaves and vegetable stock. Bring to the boil, reduce the heat and simmer over a low heat for 5 minutes.

While the laksa is cooking, put the noodles in a bowl. Cover with boiling water and leave to soak for about 10 minutes or according to the packet instructions. When the noodles are soft, but still have bite, drain well and add them to the chicken and coconut laksa sauce.

Add the fish sauce, red pepper, beansprouts, sugar snap peas and spring onion to the laksa and cook for 1 minute.

Serve family style in a large bowl and garnish with coriander leaves and chopped cashew nuts. Dish out individually according to the rule of palm (page 15).

Jennifer's tip Pad Thai noodles are available online, in some large supermarkets and Asian supermarkets. If you can't find them locally, substitute flat dried rice noodles, which is basically what they are.

I find this dish very comforting. You can use any mushrooms you like; I choose ones that have lots of flavour. It can be hard to work out what portion to give everyone, but I find two big dollops of risotto per person is about right – the total meal should be the size of two fists. Barley takes ages to cook compared to risotto rice, but persevere as it has a great texture.

Wild Mushroom Barley Risotto

Serves **4**
Preparation time **10 minutes**
Cooking time **1 hour 20 minutes**
Wheat free

INGREDIENTS	PREPARATION
1 tablespoon groundnut oil 2 shallots, peeled and finely chopped 4 garlic cloves, peeled and finely chopped	Put the groundnut oil in a non-stick pan. Add the shallots and garlic and set over a low heat. Cook for about 3 minutes until soft.
140g pearl barley	Add the barley to the pan and stir for 1 minute to coat the grains.
200ml white wine	Add the wine, bring to the boil and cook off the alcohol. This will take about 3 minutes.
1 litre chicken stock (page 27), hot	Reduce the heat and add the stock to the pan, a ladleful at a time. Stir every few minutes. When the liquid has dissolved, it is time to add another ladleful.
500g mixed mushrooms, cut into 3mm slices (I like chestnut, oyster, shiitake and porcini)	After 20 minutes, add the mushrooms to the pan. Continue to add stock and stir as before.
200g curly kale, roughly chopped	Steam the kale for a few minutes over a pan of boiling water until it is limp.
200g frozen peas	When the barley is cooked (you can tell by tasting), add the frozen peas. In total, the barley takes about 40 minutes to cook.
100g Parmesan cheese, finely grated	Turn off the heat and stir in the Parmesan.
to serve	Serve family style on the table, dishing up two fists' worth of risotto per person, with the kale either stirred through or on the side.

Jennifer's tip The better your stock, the better the dish will taste – make sure you add the stock hot to allow the other ingredients to continue cooking. To make this dish vegetarian you can use vegetable stock and substitute an alternative hard cheese for the Parmesan.

Turmeric Chicken with Spicy Tomato Aubergine

My dad is a wonderful chef and this is one of my favourite recipes that he cooks for us. He doesn't normally wear gloves to make it, so is often found with yellow stained hands – not a good look! I would suggest wearing gloves.

Serves **4**
Preparation time **20 minutes**
Marinating time **2 hours – all day**
Cooking time **45 minutes**
Wheat free, Gluten free, Dairy free
Preheat oven to 200°C/Gas 6

INGREDIENTS

1.5–2kg free-range chicken, jointed

3 large garlic cloves, peeled and crushed
1 heaped teaspoon turmeric
$1/4$ teaspoon chilli powder
juice of 1 lemon
a little chicken stock (page 27), optional

2 medium aubergines, trimmed and cut into 2–3cm pieces
$1/2$ teaspoon garam masala
pinch chilli powder

400g can chopped tomatoes
$1/2$ teaspoon ground coriander
$1/2$ teaspoon ground cumin

220g brown basmati rice

to serve

PREPARATION

Joint your chicken into drumsticks, thighs and wings (all on the bone) and cut the breast meat into a few large pieces. You can ask your butcher to do this for you if you prefer.

Mix the garlic, turmeric, chilli powder and lemon juice together in a large bowl to make a marinade. Add the chicken pieces to the bowl and stir to coat. Cover and refrigerate for at least 2 hours, but it's best to leave the chicken to marinate all day if you can, mixing it around every time you pass the refrigerator.

Transfer the marinated chicken pieces to a roasting tin, skin-side up, and roast in the oven for 45 minutes, basting halfway through cooking. If the juices in the tin are getting dry, then add a little chicken stock or water. At the end of the time, check that the thighs are cooked (see tip below), as these take the longest.

Tip the aubergine into a large bowl. Sprinkle over the garam masala and chilli powder and toss to coat. Place the aubergine in a non-stick ovenproof dish and, once your chicken has been in for 20 minutes, put the aubergines in to roast for 10 minutes.

Remove the aubergines from the oven and stir in the chopped tomatoes, coriander and cumin. Return to the oven and cook for a further 15–20 minutes.

While the chicken is cooking, bring a large pan of water to the boil. Add the rice and cook for 20–25 minutes or according to the packet instructions until tender. Drain.

Serve family style on the table and dish out individually according to the rule of palm (page 15).

Jennifer's tip To check that your chicken is cooked through, pierce a thigh with a skewer. If the juices run clear, you are good to serve up.

Spiced Coconut Prawns with Roasted Cherry Tomatoes

So simple and quick to make, the combination of wild rice, basmati rice and crunchy corn gives a wonderful texture and the flavours in the sauce surprise the palate. Serve in big, pasta-type bowls so all the saucy juice drips down into the rice. Delicious.

Serves **4**
Preparation time **15 minutes**
Cooking time **35 minutes**
Wheat free, Gluten free, Dairy free
Preheat oven to 200°C/Gas 6

INGREDIENTS

120g brown basmati rice
60g quick-cook wild rice
2 tablespoons chopped coriander

360g cherry tomatoes
320g baby corn

1 tablespoon groundnut oil
2 garlic cloves, peeled and finely chopped
2.5cm piece fresh ginger, peeled and finely chopped
1 teaspoon cumin seeds
$\frac{1}{2}$ teaspoon turmeric
$\frac{1}{2}$ green chilli, deseeded and finely chopped

240ml coconut milk
360g raw tiger prawns, shelled
600g broccoli, cut into small florets

to serve

PREPARATION

Cook the basmati and wild rice in separate pans of boiling water according to the packet instructions, about 15–25 minutes each, until tender. Drain and leave to cool slightly before stirring through the coriander.

While the rice is cooking, spread the cherry tomatoes and baby corn in a single layer in a non-stick ovenproof dish. Roast in the oven for 15–20 minutes until the tomatoes are soft and bursting and the corn is brown but still crunchy. Remove from the oven and set aside.

Heat the groundnut oil in a medium non-stick pan or wok over a medium heat. Add the garlic, ginger, cumin seeds, turmeric and chilli and sauté for 1–2 minutes without colouring.

Add the coconut milk, bring to the boil, reduce the heat and simmer, uncovered, for 7 minutes. Add the prawns, broccoli and roasted cherry tomatoes (reserving the roasted baby corn to serve) and simmer for 3–4 minutes until the prawns are just cooked and pink. The broccoli should still have bite!

Serve family style on the table and dish out individually according to the rule of palm (page 15).

Jennifer's tip This is a dish that's adaptable to whatever you have in your refrigerator. Chicken, tofu or lentils instead of prawns is an easy variation. If you can only get regular wild rice, you will need to cook it for 45 minutes to an hour, so be sure to start it off before the basmati.

This pesto evolved from an abundance of mint that grew in the streams around our farm in Ireland. I would pick it from my favourite place, up the hill. Once you've tasted this pesto, mint and fish become an obvious combination.

Sea Bream with Mint Pesto

Serves **4**
Preparation time **15 minutes**
Cooking time **20–25 minutes**
Wheat free, Gluten free
Preheat oven to 200°C/Gas 6

INGREDIENTS

720g butternut squash, peeled, deseeded and cut into bite-size pieces

40g walnuts
3 garlic cloves, peeled
100g mint leaves
100g feta cheese
1 tablespoon lemon juice

4 x 120g sea bream fillets

2 teaspoons groundnut oil
2 red onions, peeled and finely chopped
5 courgettes, trimmed, grated and excess liquid squeezed out
freshly ground black pepper

to serve
mint leaves
1 lemon, cut into 4 wedges

PREPARATION

Tip the squash into a non-stick roasting tin and roast in the oven for 15–20 minutes or until soft.

While the squash is cooking, make the pesto. Place the walnuts, garlic, mint, feta and lemon juice in a food processor and blitz to a stiff paste.

Lay a piece of baking parchment out on a work surface. Place a fish fillet in the centre and spread a quarter of the pesto over the top of the fish. Bring the edges of the baking parchment up around the fish and fold over to seal. Repeat this process for each of the remaining fillets. Place the four parcels on a baking sheet and cook in the oven for 10–12 minutes.

While the fish is cooking, heat the groundnut oil in a pan over a low heat. Add the onions and cook for 3–4 minutes until soft but not coloured. Add the courgettes and a grind of black pepper and cook over a medium–high heat for 3–4 minutes or until the courgette is tender and any liquid from the courgette is cooked out.

Mix the roasted squash and courgettes together and divide evenly between four warmed plates. Place a fish parcel on each plate, and garnish with some mint leaves and a lemon wedge.

Jennifer's tip Make sure you squeeze as much water out of the courgettes as you can before cooking them, as the water is bitter to some people's palates. The best way to do this is to place them in a clean J-cloth or tea towel and gently wring the water out.

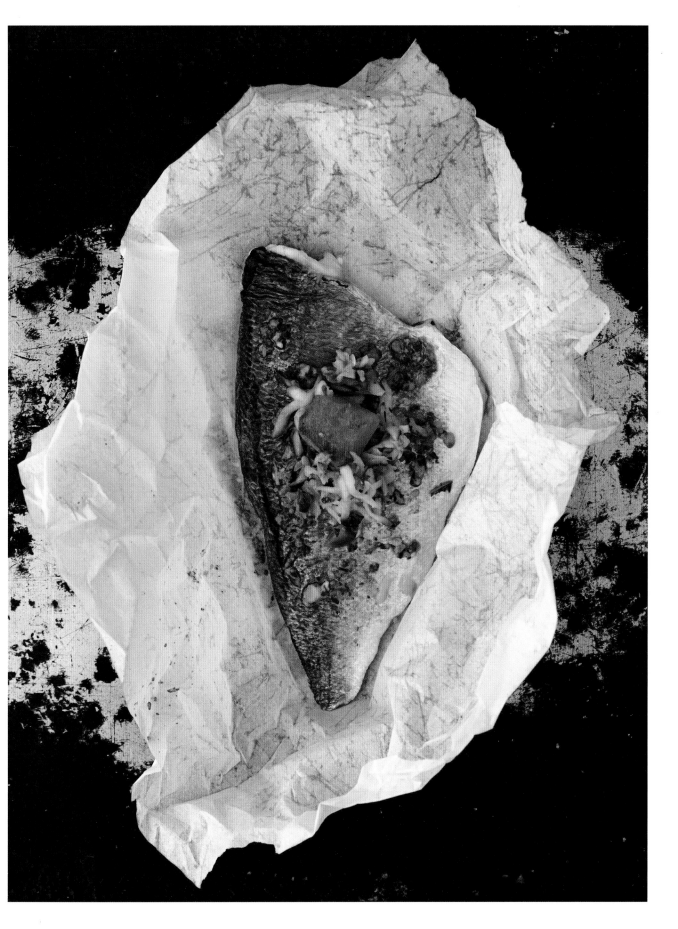

Pesto Chicken with Roasted Vegetables

This is one of our first and all-time favourite recipes. Resist the temptation to use shop-bought pesto, as it's so simple to make and the smell of fresh basil is as tantalising to the nose as it is for the taste buds. Fresh pesto will keep in the refrigerator for up to five days.

Serves **4**
Preparation time **15 minutes**
Cooking time **50 minutes**
Wheat free, Gluten free
Preheat oven to 200°C/Gas 6

INGREDIENTS

500g baby new potatoes, halved

2 red peppers, deseeded and cut into bite-size chunks
200g cherry tomatoes
3 courgettes, trimmed and cut into bite-size chunks
4 garlic cloves
small handful rosemary leaves, finely chopped
small handful thyme leaves, finely chopped

large handful basil leaves
1 tablespoon pine nuts
30g Parmesan cheese
1 tablespoon olive oil

1 teaspoon groundnut oil
4 free-range skinless chicken breasts, cut into bite-size pieces

to serve
16 basil leaves

PREPARATION

Place the potatoes in a large, shallow, nonstick ovenproof dish. Cover with foil and cook in the oven for 20 minutes.

Remove the potatoes from the oven and add the red peppers, tomatoes, courgettes, garlic, rosemary and thyme. Stir, then return to the oven, and roast, uncovered, for a further 20 minutes or until the vegetables are tender. Stir the vegetables occasionally while roasting to prevent sticking.

While the vegetables are roasting, make the pesto. Place the basil, pine nuts, Parmesan and olive oil in a food processor and blitz to a stiff paste.

Heat the groundnut oil in a pan over a medium heat. Add the chicken and stir-fry for 4–6 minutes or until it is cooked through. At the last minute, add the fresh pesto, stir and cover until you are ready to serve. Turn off the heat.

Peel the roasted garlic cloves, squash or roughly chop and mix back into the vegetables.

Either mix the pesto chicken in with the vegetables before serving or spoon the roasted vegetables around the edge of a serving platter (pour out all the juices too), place the pesto chicken into the middle and garnish with the basil leaves. Dish out individually according to the rule of palm (page 15).

Jennifer's tip If you make too much pesto, you can freeze it in ice-cube trays and pop out a cube when you want a quick dinner.

Pumpkin & Peanut Curry

This is a really yummy sauce, which you can use as a base for other vegetable, fish or meat curries if you like.

Serves **4**
Preparation time **20 minutes**
Cooking time **35 minutes**
Wheat free, Gluten free, Dairy free
Preheat oven to 200°C/Gas 6

INGREDIENTS

½ small pumpkin, peeled, deseeded and cut into bite-size pieces

320g broccoli, cut into small florets

120g brown basmati rice

1 tablespoon groundnut oil
1 small red onion, peeled and finely chopped
3 garlic cloves, peeled and finely chopped
2cm piece fresh ginger, peeled and finely chopped
1 red chilli, deseeded and finely chopped

2 teaspoons Thai green curry paste
160g chestnut mushrooms, sliced
3 tablespoons smooth peanut butter (page 49)
600ml coconut milk
juice of 2 limes
2 tablespoons tamari soy sauce

250g sugar snap peas

2 tablespoons finely chopped coriander

to serve

PREPARATION

Tip the pumpkin into a non-stick roasting tray and roast in the oven for 15–20 minutes or until soft. Remove from the oven and set aside.

Blanch the broccoli in boiling water for 2 minutes. Drain and set aside.

Cook the rice in a pan of boiling water for 20–25 minutes or according to the packet instructions until tender. Drain.

Meanwhile, heat the groundnut oil in a wok or large non-stick frying pan over a medium heat. Add the onion and cook for 2 minutes until soft but not coloured. Add the garlic, ginger and chilli and cook for a further 1 minute.

Add the curry paste and stir in the mushrooms, coating them in the paste. Stir in the peanut butter, coconut milk, lime juice and tamari and cook for 2 minutes.

Add the blanched broccoli, sugar snap peas and roasted pumpkin to the curry and simmer for 5–8 minutes. Check the seasoning and add more lime juice or tamari if needed.

Add the coriander to the curry and stir through just before you are about to serve.

Transfer the rice and curry to serving plates and serve family style on the table. Dish out individually according to the rule of palm (page 15).

Jennifer's tip Get all your ingredients prepped and ready before you start this dish as it all happens quite quickly.

This was one of the first dishes we came up with eight years ago. If you grow your own tomatoes then this recipe is great for using up all the ugly, funny-shaped ones. If you can't get this wonderful goat's cheese then a French chèvre is a good substitute – or you could use a vegetarian alternative if you prefer.

Roasted Red Peppers with St Tola Log

Serves **4**
Preparation time **15 minutes**
Cooking time **50 minutes**
Wheat free, Gluten free
Preheat oven to 200°C/Gas 6

INGREDIENTS

2 medium sweet potatoes
4 tablespoons natural yoghurt
small handful basil, finely chopped

2 plum tomatoes, quartered
2 garlic cloves, peeled and finely sliced
2 red peppers, halved and deseeded
freshly ground black pepper

240g St Tola log or another round goat's cheese, cut into 4 rounds

100g sugar snap peas
500g baby spinach leaves

to serve

PREPARATION

Place the sweet potatoes in a roasting tin and roast in the oven for 25–30 minutes until soft in the middle. Remove from the oven and, when cool enough to handle, cut in half. Scoop out some of the flesh into a bowl, leaving enough so that the potatoes still hold their shape. Mash the flesh with a fork and stir in the yoghurt and basil. Spoon the mixture back into the potato skins.

Place the tomatoes in a bowl and toss in the garlic. Place the peppers, cut-side down, and the tomatoes on a non-stick baking sheet, grind over some black pepper and roast in the oven for 10 minutes.

Remove the peppers and tomatoes from the oven. Fill the pepper halves with the roasted garlic tomatoes and top with the goat's cheese. Return the stuffed peppers and sweet potatoes to the oven and cook for 10 minutes until the goat's cheese begins to melt.

Meanwhile, steam the sugar snaps for 3–4 minutes until just cooked. Heat a large non-stick frying pan or wok over a high heat. Add the spinach and cook, stirring, for 2 minutes until the spinach is wilted.

Arrange the spinach and sugar snap peas on four serving plates. Top with a pepper half and put a stuffed sweet potato on each plate.

Jennifer's tip Wear clean rubber gloves to handle the hot potato and scoop out the flesh – it'll stop your hands getting scalded.

Paneer Cheese with Masala Spinach

Paneer cooked in this way is divine. It absorbs the flavours of the spices really well. The aim is to cook the paneer enough so that it becomes nice and soft. Try it for yourself.

Serves **4**
Preparation time **20 minutes**
Cooking time **35 minutes**
Wheat free, Gluten free, Vegetarian
Preheat oven to 200°C/Gas 6

INGREDIENTS

¹/₂ small pumpkin, peeled, deseeded and cut into bite-size pieces
¹/₄ teaspoon ground cinnamon
480g cherry tomatoes on the vine

120g brown rice
1 tablespoon finely chopped coriander

260g paneer, cut into 3cm cubes

2 teaspoons groundnut oil
¹/₂ teaspoon cumin seeds
2 garlic cloves, peeled and finely chopped
1cm piece fresh ginger, peeled and finely chopped
¹/₂ teaspoon garam masala
¹/₄ teaspoon ground cloves
1 small onion, peeled and finely chopped
¹/₂ can (200g) chopped tomatoes
pinch chilli powder

360g baby spinach leaves
100ml natural yoghurt

to serve

PREPARATION

Tip the pumpkin pieces into a large bowl. Sprinkle over the cinnamon and toss to coat. Tip the pumpkin and cherry tomatoes on the vine into a non-stick roasting tray and roast in the oven for 25 minutes or until the pumpkin is soft and the tomatoes are beginning to burst.

While the vegetables are roasting, cook the rice in a pan of boiling water for 20–25 minutes or according to the packet instructions until tender. Drain and tip back into the pan. Stir the coriander through the rice and keep warm.

While the rice is cooking, heat a griddle pan over a medium heat. Add the paneer and cook for 1 minute on each side, until golden.

Heat the groundnut oil in a non-stick pan over a high heat. Add the cumin seeds and, when they start to crackle, reduce the heat to low and add the garlic, ginger, garam masala, cloves and onion. Cook for 3–4 minutes until the onion begins to soften. Add the griddled paneer and cook, stirring, for 2 minutes. Add the chopped tomatoes and chilli powder. Bring to the boil, reduce the heat and simmer over a low heat for 15 minutes.

Heat a large wok or frying pan over a high heat. Add the spinach then stir-fry briskly for a few minutes until the spinach begins to soften and wilt. Remove from the heat and squeeze out any excess moisture. Stir the spinach and yoghurt into the simmering paneer sauce and cook for 1–2 minutes.

Serve family style on the table and dish out individually according to the rule of palm (page 15).

Jennifer's tip Take care when frying the cumin seeds as they cook very quickly. As soon as you can smell their aroma, reduce the heat and toss in the other ingredients.

Mexican Bean Pot

People don't notice that this dish is vegetarian as it's bursting with flavour. During cooking, the chilli in the sauce tastes very strong, but don't be discouraged as once served with the rice and crème fraîche the balance is perfect.

Serves **4**
Preparation time **20 minutes**
Cooking time **30 minutes**
Wheat free, Gluten free, Vegetarian
Preheat oven to 200°C/Gas 6

INGREDIENTS

1 large carrot, peeled and cut into dice
1 courgette, trimmed and cut into dice
1 small aubergine, trimmed and cut into dice
1 red pepper, deseeded and cut into dice

2 teaspoons groundnut oil
1 small onion, peeled and finely chopped
2 garlic cloves, peeled and finely chopped
1 teaspoon ground cumin
$1/4$ teaspoon chilli powder

400g can chopped tomatoes
2 tablespoons tomato purée
100ml water
400g can kidney beans, drained

160g brown rice
1 tablespoon finely chopped coriander

to serve
1 lime, cut into 4 wedges
4 tablespoons crème fraîche

PREPARATION

Tip all the vegetables into a non-stick roasting tray and roast in the oven for 20 minutes or until soft.

Heat the groundnut oil in a large heavy-based pan over a medium heat. Add the onion and cook for 3 minutes until soft but not coloured. Add the garlic, cumin and chilli powder and cook for a further 1 minute.

Tip in the tomatoes, tomato purée and water. Bring to the boil and add the roasted vegetables. Reduce the heat and simmer for 5 minutes, then add the beans and simmer gently over a low heat while you cook the rice. You may want to add more water to the sauce if it thickens up too much.

Bring a large pan of water to the boil. Add the rice and cook for 20–25 minutes or according to the packet instructions until tender. Drain and tip into a bowl. Stir the coriander through the rice.

Serve family style so that each person can portion up following the rule of palm (page 15). Garnish each plate with a lime wedge to squeeze over and a dollop of crème fraîche.

Jennifer's tip This bean pot freezes exceptionally well, so make it in large batches and freeze in portion sizes to take out as and when for convenience.

Miso Red Snapper with Asian Vegetables

This is one of my favourite ways of cooking fish as all the flavours are contained in the package and you get a real 'wow' of aroma when you open the parcel at the table.

Serves **4**
Preparation time **15 minutes**
Cooking time **20 minutes**
Wheat free, Gluten free, Dairy free
Preheat oven to 200°C/Gas 6

INGREDIENTS

5 tablespoons tamari soy sauce
4 tablespoons miso paste
3 tablespoons apple juice
1 apple, peeled, cored and grated
1 tablespoon sesame oil
4 garlic cloves, peeled and crushed

4 x 120g red snapper fillets

160g brown rice

1 teaspoon groundnut oil
350g pak choi, cut into quarters
150g mangetout, trimmed
80g baby corn, cut in half lengthways

2 teaspoons black sesame seeds

to serve
1 lime, cut into quarters

PREPARATION

In a bowl, whisk together the tamari, miso paste, apple juice, grated apple, sesame oil and garlic to make a sauce.

Lay a piece of baking parchment out on a work surface. Place a red snapper fillet in the centre, bring the edges up around the fish and pour over a little of the sauce, then bring the paper together and fold over to seal. Repeat this process for each of the remaining fillets, using up three-quarters of the sauce in total. Place the fish parcels on a baking sheet.

Cook the rice in a pan of boiling water for 20–25 minutes or according to the packet instructions until tender.

After the rice has been cooking for 10 minutes, put the fish in the oven for 10–12 minutes.

Put the pak choi, mangetout and baby corn into a non-stick wok and stir-fry for 3 minutes. Add the remaining sauce to the vegetables and stir-fry for a further 1 minute.

Drain the rice and return to the pan. Stir through the sesame seeds.

Serve family style on the table and dish out individually according to the rule of palm (page 15). Garnish each plate with a lime wedge.

Jennifer's tip You can use any white fish for this dish if you can't get hold of red snapper.

Lamb Cutlets with Roasted Balsamic Vegetables

This is an all-round simple and low-maintenance dish – a one-pot meal that, once prepared, can be left until the last minute to cook. The balsamic vinegar is a delicious addition, sweetening and thickening the roasted vegetable mixture.

Serves **4**
Preparation time **15 minutes**
Marinating time **1 hour – overnight**
Cooking time **40 minutes**
Wheat free, Gluten free, Dairy free
Preheat oven to 200°C/Gas 6

INGREDIENTS

8 lamb cutlets
small bunch **rosemary, leaves only, finely chopped**
5 garlic cloves, peeled and crushed
freshly ground black pepper

1 large red pepper, deseeded and cut into bite-size pieces
1 large yellow pepper, deseeded and cut into bite-size pieces
1 red onion, peeled and cut into wedges
8 tomatoes, cut into quarters
2 portobello mushrooms, cut into eighths
300g new potatoes, cooked
3 courgettes, cut into bite-size chunks

1 tablespoon balsamic vinegar

to serve

PREPARATION

Place the lamb cutlets in a bowl together with half the rosemary and garlic and a few twists of black pepper. Leave to marinate for at least 1 hour or overnight.

When you are ready to start cooking, place the peppers, onion, tomatoes, mushrooms, potatoes and courgettes into a large roasting tin. Scatter over the remaining rosemary leaves and garlic and season with black pepper. Roast in the oven for 30 minutes or until soft and golden. Shake the tin halfway through cooking to turn the vegetables.

Turn the oven off and preheat the grill to high. Lay the lamb cutlets on a grillpan and grill for 3 minutes on each side. Remove the meat from the grill, cover loosely with foil and leave to rest for a few minutes.

Place the roasting tin with the vegetables on the hob and drizzle over the balsamic vinegar. Cook for 2 minutes until the vinegar caramelises.

Spoon the vegetables onto warmed serving plates and arrange the lamb cutlets on top.

Jennifer's tip Bring the lamb to room temperature before cooking and either trim the fat or sear the fatty side in a very hot pan before grilling. I sometimes place the lamb on a wire rack directly over the tin of vegetables to grill (instead of using a grillpan), so that the delicious lamb juices drip onto the vegetables. If you do this, ensure that you heat the juices through fully before serving.

In the days when Gaby (now our ops manager) was head chef, she removed swordfish from our menu for ethical reasons as it was being overfished. She replaced it with kingfish, which she had grown up eating in a small fishing village on the coast of Kenya. A nice, meaty fish, it is perfect with a strong-flavoured Thai curry such as this one.

Griddled Kingfish Thai Green Curry

Serves **4**
Preparation time **20 minutes**
Cooking time **25 minutes**
Wheat free, Gluten free, Dairy free
Preheat oven to 200°C/Gas 6

INGREDIENTS

2 small butternut squash, peeled, deseeded and cut into bite-size pieces

1 teaspoon groundnut oil
2 teaspoons Thai green curry paste
1 garlic clove, peeled and finely chopped
1 tablespoon Thai fish sauce
juice of 1 lime
400ml coconut milk
2 tablespoons finely chopped coriander

400g broccoli, cut into small florets
400g sugar snap peas

4 x 100g kingfish fillets, skinned and boned
groundnut oil, for brushing

to serve

PREPARATION

Tip the squash into a non-stick roasting tray and roast in the oven for 15–20 minutes until soft. Remove from the oven and set aside.

Heat the oil in a wok or large heavy-based pan. Add the curry paste and garlic and cook for 2 minutes over a low heat. Add the fish sauce, lime juice, coconut milk and coriander and bring to just below boiling.

Tip in the broccoli and sugar snap peas, bring to the boil, reduce the heat and simmer for 5–6 minutes while you cook the fish.

Heat a heavy-based griddle pan over a high heat. Brush the kingfish fillets with groundnut oil, add to the hot pan and cook for 3 minutes, turn and cook for a further 3 minutes. Remove from the heat.

Serve family style on the table and dish out individually according to the rule of palm (page 15).

Jennifer's tip Don't be tempted to drizzle oil over the butternut squash (or any other vegetables for that matter) when roasting it. Vegetables will roast happily in their own juices. It's worth investing in a good non-stick roasting tin.

Gaby's Garlic & Ginger Chicken

Gaby came up with this dish while at uni working in the Oxford Brookes training restaurant. An amalgamation of what she deemed the best bits from other recipes, it is really flavoursome and popular with hungry blokes and gals alike.

Serves **4**
Preparation time **10 minutes**
Cooking time **25 minutes**
Wheat free, Gluten free

INGREDIENTS

160g brown basmati rice

1 tablespoon groundnut oil
6 shallots, peeled and finely chopped
3cm piece fresh ginger, peeled and finely chopped
2 garlic cloves, peeled and finely chopped
3 free-range skinless chicken breasts, cut into bite-size pieces

handful tenderstem broccoli
handful fine green beans, halved
1 courgette, trimmed and cut into julienne strips
5 tablespoons white wine
freshly ground black pepper
200ml crème fraîche
2 tablespoons tamari soy sauce

1 red pepper, deseeded and cut into julienne strips
6 chestnut mushrooms, finely sliced

to serve

PREPARATION

Bring a large pan of water to the boil, tip in the rice and cook for 20–25 minutes or according to the packet instructions until tender. Drain.

While the rice is cooking, heat the groundnut oil in a large pan. Add the shallots, ginger and garlic and cook for 2–3 minutes over a medium heat until they are beginning to soften. Add the chicken and cook for 3–5 minutes until lightly browned.

Add the broccoli, green beans, courgette and white wine. Season with black pepper. Bring to the boil. Reduce the heat, stir in the crème fraîche and tamari and simmer over a low heat for 5 minutes.

Add the red pepper strips and mushrooms to the pan and cook for a further 5–8 minutes or until the rice is cooked.

Serve family style on the table and dish out individually according to the rule of palm (page 15).

Jennifer's tip I find the best way to peel a piece of ginger is to use a teaspoon. It gets around all the knobbly bits and is much quicker than using anything else. You won't have any wastage either.

Feta Stuffed Butternut Squash

This is a perfect, colourful evening meal. The beauty of it is that you can customise your stuffing with whatever you fancy. This one is big on flavour.

Serves **4**
Preparation time **10 minutes**
Cooking time **35–45 minutes**
Wheat free, Gluten free, Vegetarian
Preheat oven to 200°C/Gas 6

INGREDIENTS

2 small butternut squash, about 500g each

1 tablespoon groundnut oil
2 onions, peeled and finely chopped
2 garlic cloves, peeled and finely chopped

280g sun-dried tomatoes in oil, drained and roughly chopped in half
4 tablespoons pumpkin seeds
200g feta cheese, lightly crumbled
2 tablespoons chopped basil

520g fine green beans, trimmed

to serve

PREPARATION

Prepare the butternut squash by cutting them in half lengthways and scooping out the seeds with a spoon. Place the squash on a non-stick baking tray and roast in the oven for 20–25 minutes or until the butternut is soft, cooked through and has a slightly coloured surface.

Meanwhile, heat the oil in a pan. Add the onions and sweat over a low heat for 4–5 minutes until they are soft and translucent. Add the garlic and cook for a further 5 minutes.

In a bowl, mix the sun-dried tomatoes, pumpkin seeds, crumbled feta, basil and cooked onions together.

Remove the butternut squash from the oven and scoop out most of the flesh so there is space for the filling. (Reserve the flesh for future use.) Fill the squash with the stuffing mixture, then return to the oven and cook for a further 10 minutes.

Steam the beans over a pan of boiling water for 4–5 minutes until tender. Remember to keep the bite.

Remove the butternut squash from the oven and serve immediately with the green beans.

Jennifer's tip Use the scooped-out butternut flesh to make the Feta & Butternut Dip on page 177.

One of the first Thai words I learnt to say while travelling around Thailand was pad Thai. It prevented me from ever going hungry as I could always fall back on a delicious steaming bowl of spicy noodles. Traditionally, pad Thai is topped with chopped peanuts, but I'm not a huge fan, so I use cashew nuts instead.

Chicken & Prawn Pad Thai

Serves **4**
Preparation time **20 minutes**
Cooking time **10 minutes**
Wheat free, Gluten free, Dairy free

INGREDIENTS

150g pad Thai rice noodles

2 tablespoons sesame oil
1 tablespoon groundnut oil
4 garlic cloves, peeled and crushed
2 red chillies, deseeded and finely chopped
200g free-range chicken breast, cut into bite-size pieces
200g raw tiger prawns, shelled
400g carrots, peeled and cut into julienne strips
500g pak choi, trimmed and quartered
300g beansprouts

3 tablespoons tamari soy sauce
3 tablespoons Thai fish sauce
1 tablespoon white wine vinegar
juice of 1 lime

to serve
70g raw unsalted cashew nuts, roughly chopped
handful coriander
1 lime, cut into 4 wedges

PREPARATION

Soak the noodles in a bowl of boiling water for about 10 minutes or according to the packet instructions. Drain and set aside.

Heat the sesame and groundnut oils in a large wok or frying pan. Add the garlic and chillies and stir-fry for a couple of seconds. Add the chicken and cook for 3 minutes. Add the prawns and cook for 2 minutes. Add the carrots, pak choi and beansprouts and stir-fry for a further 2 minutes.

Add the soaked noodles to the wok and toss together. Add the tamari, fish sauce, vinegar and lime juice and toss together, until all the flavours are combined and the wok is sizzling.

Place in the middle of a platter and scatter over the cashew nuts and coriander. Place the lime wedges around the side. Dish out individually according to the rule of palm (page 15).

Jennifer's tip This dish cooks really quickly so have all your ingredients weighed and chopped, ready to go. Make sure the noodles and pak choi are well drained before adding them to the stir fry or the dish can become soggy.

Dhal with a Cinnamon Spiced Mushroom Pilaf

Lentils are exceptionally good at absorbing flavours and are a great source of protein too. If you've never been a fan of lentils I'm confident this spicy dish will convert you.

Serves **4**
Preparation time **25 minutes**
Cooking time **45 minutes**
Wheat free, Gluten free, Vegetarian

INGREDIENTS

1 teaspoon groundnut oil
2 shallots, peeled and chopped
1 garlic clove, peeled and chopped
200g chestnut mushrooms, sliced
140g brown basmati rice
400ml boiling water
4 cloves
1 cinnamon stick
1 bay leaf

2 teaspoons groundnut oil
1 onion, peeled and finely chopped
4 garlic cloves, peeled and crushed
4cm piece fresh ginger, peeled and finely chopped

1 teaspoon ground fenugreek
1 teaspoon cumin seeds
$\frac{1}{2}$ teaspoon mustard seeds
1 teaspoon garam masala
$\frac{1}{2}$ teaspoon curry powder
1 teaspoon ground coriander

250g red lentils
$\frac{1}{2}$ can (200g) chopped tomatoes
2 tablespoons tamari soy sauce
1 litre vegetable stock (page 26), hot

400g cauliflower, cut into florets
160g baby spinach leaves
120g frozen petits pois, defrosted
2 tablespoons finely chopped coriander

25g cucumber, grated
200ml natural yoghurt
1 tablespoon finely chopped mint

to serve

PREPARATION

Heat the groundnut oil in a pan over a medium heat. Add the shallots and garlic and cook for 2–3 minutes. Add the mushrooms and cook for a further 2 minutes. Add the rice, stirring to make sure the grains are coated. Cover with the boiling water, then add the cloves, cinnamon stick and bay leaf. Bring back to the boil, reduce the heat to low and cook, covered with a lid, for 40 minutes. By this time the rice should be tender and all the liquid should have been absorbed.

While the rice is cooking, heat the groundnut oil in a pan over a medium heat. Add the onion, garlic and ginger and cook for 2 minutes until the onion is starting to soften.

Stir in the fenugreek, cumin seeds, mustard seeds, garam masala, curry powder and ground coriander and cook over a low heat for 2–3 minutes.

Add the lentils and stir to coat with the spices, then stir in the tomatoes and tamari and cook, stirring, for 2–3 minutes. Pour in half of the stock and simmer over a low heat for 10–12 minutes or until the lentils have soaked up all the liquid. Add the remaining stock, stir and simmer for a further 10–12 minutes.

When the lentils are tender with a little bite, add the cauliflower florets. After 5 minutes add the spinach, peas and finely chopped coriander to the pan and cook for a final 2–3 minutes over a low heat before serving.

Make the raita. Place the grated cucumber in a sieve and squeeze out as much of the water as possible. This will prevent the yoghurt from splitting. In a small bowl, mix together the yoghurt, mint and cucumber.

Serve family style on the table and dish out individually according to the rule of palm (page 15) with the raita served on the side.

Crispy Sea Bass Tagine with Coriander Couscous

I used to be scared of cooking sea bass as it takes so little time to cook. The trick is to have every other element of the dish prepared before you start cooking the fish. Try, if you can, to buy line-caught, wild sea bass, to ensure its sustainability.

Serves **4**
Preparation time **10 minutes**
Cooking time **25–30 minutes**
Wheat free, Dairy free

INGREDIENTS

PREPARATION

2 garlic cloves, peeled
1 tablespoon ground coriander
$^1/_2$ teaspoon ground cumin
$^1/_2$ teaspoon paprika
pinch cayenne pepper
1 tablespoon water
1 teaspoon groundnut oil

Place the garlic, coriander, cumin, paprika, cayenne, water and groundnut oil in a small food processor and blitz to make a smooth marinade.

4 x 120g sea bass fillets, skin on

Score the skin of each sea bass fillet, cutting into the flesh slightly, five or six times at about 1cm intervals. Brush both sides of the fillets with the marinade, reserving any that is not needed. Lay the fish on a plate, cover with cling film and leave to marinate while you prepare the sauce, couscous and vegetables.

2 teaspoons groundnut oil
1 small onion, peeled and chopped
3cm piece fresh ginger, peeled and grated
400g can chopped tomatoes

Heat the groundnut oil in a small non-stick pan. Add the onion and ginger and cook over a low heat for 4–5 minutes until soft but not coloured. Add the reserved marinade and the tomatoes. Bring to the boil, reduce the heat and simmer over a low heat for 10 minutes.

200g barley couscous
about 400ml vegetable stock (page 26), hot
1 tablespoon chopped coriander
1 teaspoon olive oil

Cook the couscous according to the packet instructions using vegetable stock instead of water. Stir through the chopped coriander and olive oil.

4 courgettes, trimmed and cut into bite-size chunks
6 carrots, peeled and cut into $^1/_2$cm slices
200g baby corn, cut in half lengthways

Meanwhile, steam the courgettes, carrots and baby corn over a pan of simmering water for 5 minutes until tender. Fold the vegetables through the tomato sauce.

1 teaspoon groundnut oil

Heat a frying pan until very hot, then add the oil. Lay the fish fillets in the pan skin-side down and press them down with your fingers or a fish slice to stop them curling up. Reduce the heat to medium and leave the fish to cook for 2–3 minutes, undisturbed, until you can see that the flesh has cooked two-thirds of the way up and the skin is crisp and brown. Flip the fish over and turn the heat right down, then cook on the flesh side for about 2 minutes until just cooked.

to serve

Serve family style on the table and dish out individually according to the rule of palm (page 15).

Oh-so-comforting, this twist on a traditional British cottage pie has a topping of creamy goat's cheese nestled in crushed baby potatoes. Don't feel you have to use only carrots and parsnips, as I chuck in all manner of leftover vegetables.

Cottage Pie with Baby Potato & Goat's Cheese Mash

Serves **4**
Preparation time **25 minutes**
Cooking time **1 hour 10 minutes**
Wheat free, Gluten free

INGREDIENTS

2 teaspoons groundnut oil
1 small red onion, peeled and chopped
3 garlic cloves, peeled and crushed
350g lean beef mince
small handful thyme, leaves only
3 carrots, peeled and chopped into small dice
3 parsnips, peeled and chopped into small dice

1 tablespoon tomato purée
1 tablespoon Worcestershire sauce
100ml beef stock
1 tablespoon finely chopped flat-leaf parsley
freshly ground black pepper

400g baby potatoes
100g goat's cheese
pinch grated nutmeg
1 tablespoon snipped chives

to serve

PREPARATION

Heat the groundnut oil in large saucepan. Add the onion and cook over a low heat for 5 minutes until soft and translucent. Add the garlic, beef mince and thyme and cook until the mince is browned. Add the carrots and parsnips and stir through the mince for 2 minutes.

Add the tomato purée, Worcestershire sauce and beef stock. Bring to the boil, reduce the heat and simmer, uncovered, for 1 hour if you want the beef to be really tender (you can reduce this time to 30 minutes if you are in a hurry). Check after 30 minutes and if a lot of liquid remains, increase the heat to reduce the gravy a little. Stir in the parsley and season with black pepper.

While the mince is cooking, cook the potatoes in a pan of boiling water for 15–20 minutes until tender. Drain and crush with the goat's cheese – don't overwork it as you want it to be rustic not smooth. Season with nutmeg and stir through the chives.

Preheat the grill to high.

Spoon the mince into an ovenproof dish and top with the mash. Grill for a few minutes until the mash is golden. Leave to stand for a couple of minutes before serving.

Serve family style on the table and dish out individually according to the rule of palm (page 15).

Jennifer's tip Don't overmash the baby potatoes and goat's cheese – use the back of a fork to crush your potatoes, rather than a potato masher. The top should be crisp with creamy bits of melted goat's cheese throughout.

Chicken, Feta & Leek Pie

This pie is so comforting it'll make you want to put your pyjamas on and snuggle up in front of the fire for the evening.

Serves **4**
Preparation time **15 minutes**
Cooking time **1 hour**
Wheat free, Gluten free
Preheat oven to 200°C/Gas 6

INGREDIENTS

½ **bulb garlic, unpeeled**

1 **teaspoon groundnut oil**
1 **small red onion, peeled and finely chopped**
1 **large or 2 small leeks, trimmed and thinly sliced**
3 **skinless free-range chicken breasts, cut into bite-size pieces**
2 **garlic cloves, peeled and crushed**
240g **baby spinach leaves**

100ml **single cream**
100ml **chicken stock (page 27)**
1 **bay leaf**
½ **teaspoon lemon juice**
¼ **teaspoon Dijon mustard**
¼ **teaspoon wholegrain mustard**

2 **sprigs rosemary, leaves only**
2 x 400g **cans cannellini beans, drained**
60g **feta cheese, crumbled**
200g **frozen peas, defrosted**

to serve

PREPARATION

First, roast the garlic (whole, with the skin on) in the oven for 15 minutes or until soft.

Meanwhile, heat the oil in a large frying pan. Add the onion and leeks and cook for 2 minutes until softened. Add the chicken and cook for 3–4 minutes to seal, then add the crushed garlic and spinach and cook over a high heat for a further 3 minutes or until the spinach has wilted and the liquid has evaporated.

Add the cream, chicken stock, bay leaf, lemon juice, Dijon mustard and wholegrain mustard. Bring to the boil, reduce the heat and simmer for 10 minutes. Remove from the heat.

While the leek sauce is cooking, take the garlic out of the oven and squeeze the flesh out of the roasted bulb into a mortar. Add the rosemary leaves and pound to a paste with the pestle. Tip the cannellini beans into a bowl. Add the garlic and rosemary paste and mash until smooth. Stir in the crumbled feta cheese.

Remove and discard the bay leaf from the chicken and leek mixture. Add the peas to the mix and tip into a 2-litre pie dish. Top with the cannellini bean mash and bake in the oven for 30 minutes until the mash is heated through.

Serve family style on the table and serve individually according to the rule of palm (page 15).

Jennifer's tip To clean the leeks of sand or grit, chop off the green ends, and keeping the root on, slice the leek in four lengthways. Fan out and wash under the tap, then chop the root off and slice.

Duck & Pearl Barley Cassoulet with Honey & Caraway Parsnips

This is our slant on the classic French dish cassoulet. It really is heartwarming and delicious and if there weren't other people in the room, I'd lick the plate!

Serves **4**
Preparation time **20 minutes**
Cooking time **2 hours 20 minutes**
Wheat free, Dairy free
Preheat oven to 190°C/Gas 5

INGREDIENTS

3–4 duck legs, pricked all over with a fork

1 teaspoon groundnut oil
3 large carrots, peeled and cut into large dice
3 sticks celery, cut into large dice
1 onion, peeled and finely chopped
4 garlic cloves, peeled and finely chopped

3 tablespoons tomato purée
200ml red wine
1 litre chicken (page 27) or duck stock
120g pearl barley
small bunch thyme, tied
2 sprigs rosemary
4 bay leaves
freshly ground black pepper

400g parsnips, peeled and cut into wedges
1½ teaspoons caraway seeds
1 tablespoon clear honey

240g curly kale

to serve

PREPARATION

Put the duck legs in a roasting tin and roast in the oven for 1 hour. Spoon the cooking juices into a bowl to cool, then chill. Once cold, the fat will solidify and rise to the top. Discard this and reserve the duck jelly underneath. When the duck legs are cool enough to handle, remove the skin and discard. Shred the duck meat from the bone and set aside.

Reduce the oven temperature to 180°C/Gas 4. Heat the groundnut oil in a large flameproof casserole dish. Add the carrots and cook over a medium heat until slightly coloured. Add the celery and onion and cook for 5–8 minutes until they start to caramelise, then add the garlic and cook for 2 minutes.

Stir in the tomato purée and cook for 2 minutes. Add the red wine, bring to the boil and scrape all the sediment off the base and sides of the pan to deglaze. Add the chicken stock, reserved duck jelly, pearl barley, thyme, rosemary and bay leaves. Season with black pepper. Bring back to the boil, cover and transfer to the oven for 40 minutes. Add the shredded duck meat and cook for a further 15 minutes.

Meanwhile, tip the parsnips into a non-stick roasting tin. Sprinkle with caraway seeds and drizzle with the honey. Roast in the oven for 20 minutes until soft.

Just before serving, steam the kale over a pan of boiling water for 5 minutes.

Serve family style and dish out according to the rule of palm (page 15).

Jennifer's tip Don't be tempted to cook the duck legs in the cassoulet as although it's traditional and quicker that way, the legs are very high in fat, which needs to be drained off while saving the delicious duck jelly which forms part of the stock.

Roast Beef with Home-made Horseradish Sauce

Serves **4**
Preparation time **15 minutes**
Cooking time **55 minutes**
Wheat free, Gluten free
Preheat oven to 200°C/Gas 6

This book wouldn't be complete without my family recipe for roast beef that we enjoy at the weekend. So often, the vegetables served with a roast are quite dreary and don't stand up to the meat – that's not the case here I can assure you.

INGREDIENTS

500g beef fillet

300ml chicken stock (page 27)
4 garlic cloves
handful rosemary

400g baby potatoes, skin on
2 teaspoons groundnut oil
2 sprigs rosemary, finely chopped

$1/4$ teaspoon cumin seeds
$1/4$ teaspoon coriander seeds
400g parsnips, peeled and cut into wedges
1 teaspoon clear honey

25g fresh horseradish
$1/2$ teaspoon Dijon mustard
$1/2$ tablespoon white wine vinegar
75ml crème fraîche

100ml red wine

400g carrots, peeled and sliced
150ml orange juice
2 tablespoons chopped parsley

400g cavolo nero, kale or other greens

to serve

PREPARATION

Put the beef into a roasting tin and roast in the oven for 30–35 minutes, for medium-rare, basting after 15 minutes.

Meanwhile, put the stock, garlic and rosemary in a pan and bring to the boil over a high heat. Then turn the heat right down to keep the stock warm (this is for your gravy).

Ten minutes before the beef is ready to come out the oven, coat the potatoes with the groundnut oil and rosemary, tip them into a non-stick roasting tin and roast in the oven for 25–30 minutes until tender.

Heat a small non-stick frying pan over a high heat. Add the cumin and coriander seeds and dry-fry for 30 seconds. When the seeds start to crackle, remove them from the heat and transfer to a bowl with the parsnips and honey. Toss together to coat the parsnips, then tip them into a non-stick roasting tin and roast in the oven for 20 minutes.

Make the horseradish sauce. Peel and finely grate the horseradish and whisk it together with the mustard, vinegar and crème fraîche. Spoon into a serving bowl.

When the beef is cooked, transfer it to a warmed serving plate, cover with foil and leave to rest for 15 minutes. Place the roasting tin over a low heat and add the wine to deglaze the pan, scraping all the sediment off the base and sides of the tin. Bring the juices to the boil, add the hot stock, squash the garlic into the gravy and leave to reduce by half. Strain to remove the rosemary before serving.

Tip the carrots into a pan and pour over the orange juice. Bring to the boil, cover and cook for 15 minutes until tender, then drain and return the carrots to the pan. Add the parsley and toss together.

Steam the cavolo nero over a pan of simmering water for 3–4 minutes until wilted.

Serve family style on the table and dish out individually according to the rule of palm (page 15).

SNACKS

Snacks

WE ALL LOVE SNACKING and you can stop feeling guilty as it's an essential part of a well-balanced diet. Not only do nutritious, healthy snacks stave off hunger pangs but they also keep your blood sugar levels stable, helping to keep energy levels up and the brain alert. For those worried about it affecting their waistline, don't be; going without food for a long period of time can encourage the body to store fat, slow metabolism and can actually be detrimental to weight loss.

A healthy snack should always contain a good source of protein. Protein is essential for healthy growth and development, bone health, the immune system and brain function. It also helps with blood sugar control to avoid energy slumps and cravings for sweet things.

At The Pure Package we find it best to have a healthy snack mid-way between breakfast and lunch, and again between lunch and dinner.

One of your snacks each day should be fresh fruit with a combination of raw nuts or seeds. In our three-week plan (pages 208–213) you will find recommended combinations, and you can read more about the benefits of these combinations in our grab snacks section (page 206).

The other snack, and there are recipes for these in this section, can be a mix of all sorts – from fruit yoghurts, dips and crudités to sweeter, more indulgent snacks (some of which are great as desserts) like our famous chocolate mousse and muffins.

I always make sure I snack regularly, and these recipes are all designed to be eaten on the run, at your desk, at the gym… they are also very easy and quick to put together.

Poached Eggs with Asparagus

A great alternative to dips and chips, this recipe is the result of unexpected guests arriving when the cupboards were bare of canapés. I simply poached some fresh hen's eggs and served with asparagus. It's something our guests have been demanding ever since and is particularly lovely with drinks in summertime.

Serves **4**
Preparation time **5 minutes**
Cooking time **6 minutes**
Wheat free, Gluten free, Dairy free, Vegetarian

INGREDIENTS

12 asparagus spears, trimmed

4 free-range eggs, at room temperature

to serve

PREPARATION

Steam the asparagus spears over a pan of simmering water for 3 minutes.

Bring another small pan filled three-quarters full of water to just below boiling point, then add your eggs. If you prefer, you can break each one into a cup and pour into the water – this way you will have a nice neat egg. Remove the eggs from the water with a slotted spoon.

Serve the poached eggs on serving plates and dip the asparagus spears into the runny yolk.

Jennifer's tip When poaching eggs it's important that they are as fresh as possible. Lead the way and show your guests how to eat by tucking in first.

Fresh Spring Rolls with Sweet Chilli Sauce

Spring rolls have always just been a fried thing in Chinese restaurants to me, so I was delighted when I came across these fresh versions in Laos. Clean and crunchy, sweet and sour, I love them!.

Serves **4**
Preparation time **10 minutes**
Cooking time **20 minutes**
Wheat free, Gluten free, Dairy free

INGREDIENTS

1 tablespoon lime juice
1 tablespoon Thai fish sauce
2 teaspoons clear honey
1 tablespoon water
1 small garlic clove, peeled and crushed
½ red chilli, deseeded and finely sliced

50g packet rice flour pancakes
25g vermicelli rice noodles

¼ cucumber, deseeded and shredded
1 small carrot, peeled and shredded
18 coriander leaves
12 mint leaves
4 large cooked prawns, cut in half lengthways

to serve

PREPARATION

To make the dipping sauce, whisk together the lime juice, fish sauce, honey, water, garlic and chilli and heat in a pan to infuse the flavours gently for 20 minutes. Do not boil. Leave to cool.

Soak the rice flour pancakes according to the packet instructions or in boiling water for 30 seconds. Remove and cool on a clean tea towel. Put the noodles in a heatproof bowl and cover with boiling water. Leave to soak until just tender, about 5 minutes or according to the packet instructions. Drain and cut into 2cm strips.

Lay a rice pancake on a board and arrange some noodles, cucumber, carrot and herbs about a third of the way into the centre of the pancake. Top with two prawn halves. Fold the sides of the pancake in over the filling (or leave one end open if you prefer), then roll up lengthways to make a cigar. Repeat with the remaining pancakes and filling mixture to make four in total.

If you have sealed your spring rolls at both ends, cut them in half on the diagonal. If you've left them open at one end then they're best kept whole. Arrange on serving plates, ready to dunk into the dipping sauce.

Jennifer's tip Feel free to swap your fillings – beansprouts, mangetout and duck also work well. Rice flour pancakes are a great storecupboard ingredient. I buy them once a year from a Chinese supermarket as they keep for ages and are so useful when it comes to last-minute canapés.

Sun-dried Tomato & Bean Dip with Sugar Snap Peas

I assure you that just because this recipe is easy and made from storecupboard ingredients, it doesn't mean it's not tasty. Simple and really delicious, it works well as a baked potato topping too.

Serves **4**
Preparation time **6 minutes**
Wheat free, Gluten free, Dairy free, Vegetarian

INGREDIENTS

40g sun-dried tomatoes in oil
¹/₂ can (200g) cannellini beans

to serve
500g sugar snap peas

PREPARATION

Drain the sun-dried tomatoes and cannellini beans, reserving the oil from the tomatoes.

Add the tomatoes and beans to a food processor and blitz to a stiff paste. With the motor running, slowly add some of the drained sun-dried tomato oil until you get the right consistency. The dip shouldn't be runny so you will only need about a tablespoon.

Spoon into a small serving bowl and serve with the sugar snap peas for a nice crunch.

Jennifer's tip Substitute the sugar snaps with corn chips or other raw vegetables if you fancy.

Hummus with Corn Chips

Hummus is one of those things that takes minutes to make from storecupboard ingredients. It's not the most visually appealing dip, but we've discovered that if you serve it in a black bowl topped with a few pomegranate kernels it takes on a whole different image and looks oh-so-appetising. It's also a very versatile dish: there are three variations on this basic hummus recipe on the following pages.

Serves **4**
Preparation time **10 minutes**
Wheat free, Gluten free, Dairy free, Vegetarian

INGREDIENTS

400g can chickpeas, drained
1 tablespoon tahini
pinch ground cumin
1 tablespoon olive oil
juice of $1/2$ lemon
up to 3 tablespoons vegetable stock (page 26) or water

to serve
kernels from $1/2$ pomegranate
300g corn chips

PREPARATION

Put the chickpeas into a food processor, add the tahini, cumin and olive oil and blitz to a stiff paste. With the motor running, slowly add the lemon juice and some vegetable stock or water to get it to the consistency you prefer.

Spoon the hummus into a small serving bowl, sprinkle the pomegranate kernels on top and serve with the corn chips.

Jennifer's tip Cut the pomegranate in half, then hold cut-side down and tap the top with a spoon. The kernels will fall out undamaged.

Roasted Red Pepper Hummus with Celery & Radishes

Serves 4
Preparation time 15 minutes
Cooking time 25 minutes
Wheat free, Gluten free, Dairy free, Vegetarian
Preheat oven to 200°C/Gas 6

INGREDIENTS

1 red pepper, halved
1 small garlic clove, unpeeled

400g can chickpeas, drained
1 tablespoon tahini
juice of ¹/₂ lemon
¹/₂ small red chilli, deseeded and
finely chopped
1 tablespoon olive oil
up to 3 tablespoons vegetable stock
(page 26) or water

to serve
8 sticks celery, cut into batons
8 radishes, leaves on

PREPARATION

Place the red pepper and garlic on a baking sheet, skin-side up and roast in the oven for 20–25 minutes or until the skin of the pepper is blackened and blistered. Remove the pepper from the oven, put it straight into a freezer bag and seal, as the steam helps to loosen the skin. When cool enough to handle, peel the pepper and garlic and discard the skins.

Put the chickpeas into a food processor, add the roasted pepper flesh, roasted garlic, tahini, lemon juice and chopped chilli and blitz to a stiff paste. With the motor running, slowly add the olive oil and blend until smooth, adding some vegetable stock or water if needed to get it to the consistency you prefer.

Spoon the hummus into a small serving bowl and serve with the celery and radishes.

Lemon & Coriander Hummus with Carrot Sticks

Serves **4**
Preparation time **10 minutes**
Wheat free, Gluten free, Dairy free, Vegetarian

INGREDIENTS

400g can chickpeas, drained
1 tablespoon tahini
juice of 1/2 lemon
1 tablespoon olive oil
up to 3 tablespoons vegetable stock
(page 26) or water
1/2 tablespoon finely chopped coriander

to serve

8 coriander leaves
grated zest of 1/2 lemon
400g carrots, peeled and
cut into batons

PREPARATION

Put the chickpeas into a food processor, add the tahini and lemon juice and blitz to a stiff paste. With the motor running, slowly add the olive oil and blend until smooth, adding some vegetable stock or water if needed to get it to the consistency you prefer. Transfer the hummus to a bowl and stir in the finely chopped coriander. Taste it to decide if you want to add a touch more lemon juice or coriander.

Spoon the hummus into a small serving bowl. Place the coriander leaves on the top and garnish with grated lemon zest. Serve with the carrot sticks.

Sun-dried Tomato Hummus with Cucumber & Pepper Sticks

Serves 4
Preparation time 10 minutes
Wheat free, Gluten free, Dairy free, Vegetarian

INGREDIENTS

400g can chickpeas, drained
70g sun-dried tomatoes in oil
$^1/_4$ teaspoon smoked paprika
1 tablespoon finely chopped basil

to serve

1 yellow pepper, deseeded and cut
into batons
$^1/_2$ cucumber, halved, deseeded and
cut into batons

PREPARATION

Put the chickpeas into a food processor, add the sun-dried tomatoes (reserving the oil) and paprika and blitz to a stiff paste. With the motor running, add the reserved sun-dried tomato oil a little at a time and blend until smooth. You may not need all of the oil, as the hummus should not be runny. Transfer to a bowl and stir in the basil.

Spoon the hummus into a small serving bowl and serve with the pepper and cucumber batons.

Artichoke & Bean Dip with Sugar Snap Peas

This yummy dip makes the perfect afternoon snack and conjures up dreams of holidaying in the Mediterranean. Dip away!

Serves **5–6**
Preparation time **5 minutes**
Wheat free, Gluten free, Dairy free, Vegetarian

INGREDIENTS

280g artichoke hearts in oil
400g can cannellini beans

small handful of flat-leaf parsley, leaves only
juice of ½ lemon

to serve
500g sugar snap peas

PREPARATION

Drain the artichoke hearts and cannellini beans.

Place the artichoke hearts in a food processor with the cannellini beans, parsley and lemon juice. Blitz to a smooth paste.

Spoon the dip into a small serving bowl and serve with the sugar snap peas for a nice crunch.

Jennifer's tip Substitute the sugar snaps with corn chips or oatcakes or any other raw vegetables if you fancy. This can be kept in the refrigerator for up to four days.

Feta & Butternut Dip with Oatcakes

This is a great dip for using up leftover roasted butternut squash or pumpkin. It works really well as an accompaniment to grilled meat and fish too.

Serves 4
Preparation time 15 minutes
Cooking time 20–30 minutes
Wheat free, Vegetarian
Preheat oven to 200°C/Gas 6

INGREDIENTS

200g butternut squash, peeled, deseeded and cut into bite-size pieces

40g feta cheese
1 teaspoon harissa

to serve
12 oatcakes

PREPARATION

Tip the butternut squash onto a non-stick baking sheet and roast in the oven for 15–20 minutes or until soft. Leave to cool.

Place the butternut into a food processor with the feta cheese and harissa and blitz to a smooth paste.

Spoon the dip into a serving bowl. Serve with the oatcakes.

Jennifer's tip To save time peeling and chopping, simply roast the butternut squash halved or quartered with its skin on and scoop out the flesh once it's cooked.

Tomato Salsa with Corn Chips

Serves 4
Preparation time 10 minutes
Infusing time 1 hour or more
Wheat free, Gluten free, Dairy free, Vegetarian

Fresh, flavourful, versatile and so quick to prepare, use ripe tomatoes and the freshest of herbs to make this salsa. It is only going to be as good as your ingredients.

INGREDIENTS

4–5 large plum tomatoes, peeled, deseeded and chopped into small dice
1 teaspoon snipped chives
1 teaspoon balsamic vinegar
1 teaspoon olive oil
handful basil, finely chopped

to serve
300g corn chips

PREPARATION

Put the tomatoes into a large bowl and add the chives, vinegar, olive oil and basil. Stir to combine, cover and leave to stand at room temperature for at least 1 hour for the flavours to infuse.

Spoon the tomato salsa into a small serving bowl and serve with the corn chips.

Jennifer's tip To peel tomatoes, score a cross in the skin of the base of each tomato. Place in a bowl and pour over a kettle of boiling water. Leave for a few seconds until the skin near the cross starts to curl. Remove with a slotted spoon and immediately plunge into cold water, then peel off the skin.

This is our twist on the standard guacamole. Avocados are a good source of Vitamin E which is renowned for having excellent moisturising properties. A good way to test if they are ripe is to give them a shake – if you can hear the stone rattling around they are good to use.

Pea & Avocado Guacamole

Serves **4**
Preparation time **10 minutes**
Wheat free, Gluten free, Vegetarian

INGREDIENTS

80g frozen peas, defrosted
1/2 avocado, peeled and stoned
1 tablespoon lime juice
1 red chilli, deseeded and finely chopped
2 tablespoons Greek yoghurt
pinch ground cumin
pinch ground coriander

1 plum tomato, peeled, deseeded and finely chopped
small handful coriander, finely chopped

to serve
4 sticks celery, trimmed and cut into batons
160g carrots, peeled and cut into batons

PREPARATION

Put the peas in a food processor with the avocado, lime juice, chilli, yoghurt, ground cumin and ground coriander. Blitz to a smooth paste.

Transfer to a bowl and fold through the chopped tomato and chopped coriander.

Serve the guacamole in small serving bowls with the raw vegetables.

Jennifer's tip To make your avocado easier to peel, dip the avocado into a bowl of boiling water for 10 seconds then remove. The skin will peel away from the flesh with ease; it may also keep the avocado from going black as quickly.

Baba Ganoush with Oatcakes

A delicious spiced aubergine dip, this baba ganoush works really well with roast or grilled lamb too. Don't be tempted to slather the aubergine in salt as so many recipes tell you to do. There really is no need.

Serves 4
Preparation time 15 minutes
Cooking time 20–30 minutes
Wheat free, Vegetarian
Preheat oven to 200°C/Gas 6

INGREDIENTS

1 large aubergine, trimmed
1 garlic clove, peeled and quartered

1 tablespoon tahini
1 tablespoon lemon juice
$\frac{1}{2}$ teaspoon ground cumin
2 tablespoons natural yoghurt
freshly ground black pepper

to serve
1 teaspoon olive oil
small handful flat-leaf parsley, chopped
8 oatcakes

PREPARATION

Cut the aubergine in half. Using the tip of a knife, make two cuts in the flesh of each half and bury a piece of garlic in each slit. Place on a non-stick baking sheet and roast in the oven for 20–30 minutes or until the skin is blistered and the flesh is soft. When cool enough to handle, scoop out the flesh along with the garlic.

Put the aubergine flesh and garlic into a food processor and pulse to a mash (do not blitz to a purée). Transfer to a bowl and stir in the tahini, lemon juice, ground cumin and yoghurt. Season with black pepper.

Spoon the baba ganoush into a serving bowl. Drizzle over the olive oil, scatter with parsley and serve with the oatcakes.

Jennifer's tip Don't overdo the cumin or you will overwhelm the aubergine flavour.

Ginger Infused Fruit & Seed Salad

Beautifully clean and delicious, this recipe might look like a plain fruit salad on paper, but once you taste it, the ginger mingles with the fruit on your palate and is utterly divine.

Serves 4
Preparation time **5 minutes**
Infusing time **30 minutes – all day**
Wheat free, Gluten free, Vegetarian

INGREDIENTS

2 papayas, peeled, deseeded and sliced
4 kiwi fruit, peeled and sliced
1 piece preserved stem ginger, finely chopped

to serve
60g pumpkin seeds
1 tablespoon black sesame seeds
4 tablespoons natural yoghurt

PREPARATION

Mix the papaya and kiwi together with the chopped stem ginger. Leave for 30 minutes, or all day if you have time, for the flavours to infuse.

Arrange the papaya and kiwi on four serving plates. Sprinkle over the pumpkin and sesame seeds. Top with a spoonful of yoghurt.

Jennifer's tip A good fruit salad depends on the quality and ripeness of the fruit. If your fruit is underripe, put the papayas in a paper bag to ripen and the kiwi fruit in a freezer bag with an apple. The exposure to ethylene from the apple hastens the ripening.

Rhubarb & Ginger Jelly

Perfect for the spring when field-grown rhubarb really comes into its own. This is yummy as a dessert too and the rhubarb and ginger work really well together.

Serves **4**
Preparation time **10 minutes**
Cooking time **20 minutes**
Setting time **4 hours**
Wheat free, Gluten free, Vegetarian

INGREDIENTS

150g rhubarb, trimmed and cut into 2.5cm pieces
1 piece preserved stem ginger, finely chopped
1 tablespoon clear honey
½ teaspoon vanilla paste

200ml orange juice
VegeSet or agar-agar powder

100ml crème fraîche
finely grated zest of ¼ orange

to serve
1 piece preserved stem ginger, finely chopped

PREPARATION

Tip the rhubarb into a medium heavy-based saucepan with the ginger, honey and vanilla paste. Cook over a very low heat for 10–15 minutes to allow the rhubarb to poach in its own juices until soft.

Mix the cold orange juice and VegeSet or agar-agar powder together in a small heavy-based pan, following the packet instructions for the correct quantity of gelling agent. Whisk together and then turn on the heat. Heat slowly and stir until small bubbles begin to appear. Turn off the heat and leave to cool slightly. Stir in the poached rhubarb and juices. Spoon into four serving glasses or ramekins. Leave to cool slightly before chilling in the refrigerator for 4 hours.

Mix the crème fraîche and grated orange zest together in a small bowl until well combined.

When set, remove the jellies from the refrigerator and delicately dollop the crème fraîche on the top. Sprinkle with chopped stem ginger.

Jennifer's tip Don't let your orange juice and VegeSet or agar-agar powder mix boil. It is important to take it off the heat as soon as you see small bubbles appearing.

Summer Pudding Jelly with Vanilla & Honey Greek Yoghurt

Make this jelly in the summer using seasonal British berries and there will be no need to add honey to your yoghurt topping. Substitute the berries with other fruit when out of season.

Serves 4
Preparation time **5 minutes**
Cooking time **6 minutes**
Setting time **1–2 hours**
Wheat free, Gluten free, Vegetarian

INGREDIENTS

400ml grape juice
VegeSet or agar-agar powder

50g raspberries
50g strawberries, hulled and halved
50g blueberries

100ml Greek yoghurt
$1/4$ teaspoon vanilla paste
1 teaspoon clear honey

to serve
4 mint leaves

PREPARATION

Bring the grape juice to the boil in a small heavy-based pan. Stir in the VegeSet or agar-agar powder (following the packet instructions for the correct quantity of gelling agent) and simmer for 2–3 minutes, stirring until dissolved. Remove from the heat and leave to cool a little until the mixture begins to thicken.

As soon as the jelly starts to set, divide the raspberries, strawberries and blueberries between four ramekins or dessert glasses. Pour over the jelly and leave to chill in the refrigerator for 1–2 hours to set firm.

Mix the Greek yoghurt, vanilla paste and honey together in a small bowl until well combined.

Remove the jellies from the refrigerator and spread the yoghurt over the top in a layer. Decorate each glass with a mint leaf.

Jennifer's tip VegeSet is just as good as agar-agar and it is cheaper. You can buy it at www.justwholefoods.co.uk. If you are not vegetarian, you could use gelatine instead — you will need three leaves to set this quantity of jelly.

Stewed Plum Yoghurt

This yoghurt is an amazing pink colour, and with my three young daughters, it is a huge hit in our house.

Serves **4**
Preparation time **5 minutes**
Cooking time **15–20 minutes**
Wheat free, Gluten free, Vegetarian

INGREDIENTS

500g plums, halved and stoned
2–3 tablespoons grape juice
$\frac{1}{4}$ teaspoon ground cinnamon
50ml water

50ml Greek yoghurt
250ml natural yoghurt

to serve

PREPARATION

Place the plums in a small pan with the grape juice, cinnamon and water. Bring to the boil, cover and cook over a low heat for 10–15 minutes until soft. Drain and mash the plums with a fork or potato masher.

Mix the Greek yoghurt and natural yoghurt together and stir in the plums.

Portion out individually into dishes or cups.

Jennifer's tip Plums contain amino acid tryptophan, which apparently the body uses to produce serotonin, a mood enhancer. So not only does this yoghurt look great, it may also make you feel great!

Stewed Pears with Coconut Yoghurt

The combination of flavours and the contrast of hot pears and cold yoghurt make this dessert fit for a dinner party.

Serves **4**
Preparation time **10 minutes**
Cooking time **35–40 minutes**
Wheat free, Gluten free, Vegetarian

INGREDIENTS

1 tablespoon sultanas
2 tablespoons red grape juice

4 pears, peeled, cored and cut into halves or quarters
120ml apple juice
100ml red grape juice

25g coconut flakes

100ml Greek yoghurt
1/2 teaspoon vanilla paste

to serve

PREPARATION

Place the sultanas in a cup. Pour over the grape juice and leave to soak while you poach the pears.

Place the pears in a heavy-based pan. Pour over the apple and grape juices and bring to the boil. Reduce the heat and simmer for 25–30 minutes until the pears are tender. Remove the pears with a slotted spoon and set aside. Return the pan to the heat and boil over a high heat until the juice is reduced by half, to a thick syrup. Remove from the heat.

While the pears are poaching, heat a non-stick frying pan over a medium heat. Add the coconut flakes and dry-fry for 30 seconds, tossing the pan until golden. Watch carefully as they burn easily. Remove from the heat.

Mix the Greek yoghurt and vanilla paste together.

Divide the poached pears between four serving bowls. Pour over the syrup and the sultanas. Top with the vanilla yoghurt and scatter with the toasted coconut.

Jennifer's tip If you can't get hold of red grape juice, don't panic, just replace it with white or rosé wine.

Stewed Fig Yoghurt

I love figs and particularly like the crunchy texture of the seeds in this yoghurt recipe. We have figs growing in our garden and always make the most of them, as the season is over in a flash. I think that no two figs are the same and when you cut into them, it's like catching the sunset on different days.

Serves **4**
Preparation time **5 minutes**
Cooking time **15 minutes**
Wheat free, Gluten free, Vegetarian

INGREDIENTS

2–3 fresh figs
1 small orange, halved
2 cloves
enough water to cover
60g ready-to-eat dried figs

100ml Greek yoghurt
100ml natural yoghurt

to serve
1 additional fresh fig, cut into quarters

PREPARATION

Begin by cutting the hard stems off the fresh figs, then place them in a small pan with the orange and cloves. Cover with water and bring to the boil. Turn the heat down, cover and cook over a low heat for about 10 minutes until the figs are soft. Remove the figs with a slotted spoon, reserving the liquid. Place the cooked figs in a food processor with the dried figs and blitz to a paste. With the motor running, slowly add some of the reserved cooking liquid and blitz to a smooth purée. You may not need to add all of the liquid.

Mix the Greek and natural yoghurt together and mix in the stewed figs.

Divide the stewed fig yoghurt between four serving bowls and top each with a fresh fig quarter.

Jennifer's tip Don't forget to remove the cloves from the cooking liquid before puréeing, or their flavour will overpower the figs.

Stewed Spiced Apple Yoghurt

This is so much tastier than buying a sugar- or sweetener-laden supermarket yoghurt. You can really taste the goodness and you get to control what you put in there.

Serves **4**
Preparation time **5 minutes**
Cooking time **15–20 minutes**
Wheat free, Gluten free, Vegetarian
Preheat oven to 180°C/Gas 4

INGREDIENTS

**3 large apples, peeled, cored and roughly chopped into 3cm pieces
pinch ground cinnamon
pinch five spice powder
1 star anise**

**200ml Greek yoghurt
100ml natural yoghurt**

to serve

PREPARATION

Mix the apples with the cinnamon, five spice powder and star anise. Tip into an ovenproof dish and roast in the oven for 15–20 minutes or until soft.

Mix the two types of yoghurt together then stir in the apples, leaving out the star anise.

Divide the yoghurt between four bowls.

Jennifer's tip If you like your yoghurt a bit tart, use one Bramley apple with two sweeter apples like Braeburn.

Cinnamon Spiced Plums

These yummy spiced plums are as delicious served warm as they are cold and make a great spread to put on toasted rye bread too.

Serves 4
Preparation time 5 minutes
Cooking time 20–30 minutes
Wheat free, Gluten free, Dairy free, Vegetarian
Preheat oven to 180°C/Gas 4

INGREDIENTS

8 plums, halved and stoned
4 tablespoons red wine
¼ teaspoon ground cinnamon
4 cardamom pods
½ teaspoon five spice powder
3 tablespoons water

to serve
20g sunflower seeds
20g pumpkin seeds

PREPARATION

Pack the plums, cut-side up, into an ovenproof dish so they fit snugly together. Put the wine into a jug, add the cinnamon, cardamom pods, five spice powder and water and stir together. Pour over the plums and roast in the oven for 20–30 minutes until soft. Remove from the oven and serve immediately if you want them warm, or leave to cool and then chill if the plan is to eat them cold.

Divide the spiced plums evenly between four serving bowls and scatter over the sunflower and pumpkin seeds.

Jennifer's tip Feel free to experiment with a mixture of plums, greengages, damsons and mirabelles. You can also vary the spices. The roasted plums can be kept in the refrigerator for up to three days.

Baked Peaches with Ricotta

Serves **4**
Preparation time **5 minutes**
Cooking time **20–30 minutes**
Wheat free, Gluten free, Vegetarian
Preheat oven to 180°C/Gas 4

This recipe is a great way to use up any bruised or blemished fruit that you may have lying around. I had some bruised peaches I didn't want to go to waste, so I baked them and this yummy recipe evolved.

INGREDIENTS

4 peaches, halved and stoned
3 tablespoons white wine
½ teaspoon ground cinnamon
4 cardamom pods
½ teaspoon five spice powder
4 tablespoons water

3 tablespoons ricotta
3 tablespoons natural yoghurt

to serve

PREPARATION

Pack the peaches, cut-side up, into an ovenproof dish so they fit snugly together. Put the wine into a jug, add the cinnamon, cardamom, five spice and water and stir together. Pour over the peaches and roast in the oven for 30–35 minutes until soft. Remove from the oven and serve immediately if you want them warm or leave to chill if the plan is to eat them cold.

Mix the ricotta and yoghurt together.

Divide the spiced peaches evenly between four serving bowls, drizzling some of the cooking liquid over them and top with the ricotta and yoghurt mix.

Jennifer's tip Feel free to experiment with a mixture of nectarines and plums too. The baked peaches can be kept in the refrigerator for up to three days.

Chocolate Mousse

I considered excluding this recipe from the book as it is so simple to make, but I have had so many requests for it, I figured there might be a witch hunt if I didn't pop it in here! It is a recipe I really love and it is also good for you as chocolate is a rich source of antioxidants. Eat as a mousse or pop it into the freezer to make a lovely ice cream. By topping with raspberries or hazelnuts you give it that extra crunch and flavour.

Serves 4
Preparation time 5 minutes
Cooking time 10 minutes
Chilling time 2 hours – overnight
Wheat free, Gluten free, Vegetarian

INGREDIENTS

100g plain dark chocolate (at least 70% cocoa solids), broken into pieces
1 teaspoon cocoa powder

8 free-range egg whites, at room temperature

to serve
cocoa powder, for dusting

PREPARATION

Melt the chocolate in a heatproof bowl set over a saucepan of gently simmering water, making sure the base of the bowl isn't touching the water. Leave to cool slightly and then stir in the cocoa powder.

The secret to this recipe is to have the temperature of the chocolate and eggs similar so nothing is shocked. Whisk the egg whites in a clean, dry and grease-free bowl until they form soft peaks, then fold them into the cooled melted chocolate.

Spoon the mixture into small cups or ramekins and chill in the refrigerator for 2 hours or overnight.

Dust with a little cocoa powder before serving.

Jennifer's tip You can use pasteurised egg whites for this recipe (find them in the chiller section of larger supermarkets), which are generally safer for pregnant women – and it means the mousse will keep longer.

Banana, Date & Apricot Muffins

These muffins have a really good natural sweetness from the honey and sultanas, and the best thing is that my kids love them so it's the perfect way to get them to eat more fruit. 'More!' is their verdict.

Makes **12**
Preparation time **15 minutes**
Cooking time **30 minutes**
Wheat free, Gluten free, Dairy free, Vegetarian
Preheat oven to 160°C/Gas 3

INGREDIENTS

150g brown rice flour or ground rice
2 teaspoons bicarbonate of soda
2 teaspoons gluten-free baking powder
2 teaspoons ground cinnamon
120g sultanas
120g ready-to-eat dried apricots, chopped
120g ready-to-eat dates, chopped
40g pecan nuts, chopped

2 tablespoons clear honey
80ml sunflower oil
150ml apple juice
4 ripe bananas, peeled and mashed
2 apples, peeled, cored and grated
2 free-range eggs, at room temperature, beaten

to serve

PREPARATION

Line a 12-hole muffin tin with paper muffin cases. Sift the rice flour, bicarbonate of soda, baking powder and cinnamon into a large bowl. Stir in the sultanas, apricots, dates and pecan nuts.

In a separate bowl, mix the honey, sunflower oil, apple juice, mashed banana, grated apple and eggs together. Make a well in the centre of the dry ingredients and pour in the wet mixture. Stir gently with a wooden spoon to combine. Divide the batter equally between the 12 muffin cases and bake in the oven for 30 minutes or until a skewer inserted into the centre comes out clean. Remove from the oven and leave to cool on a wire rack.

Serve warm or cold.

Jennifer's tip These muffins get better with age – try them a couple of days after baking and you will be very pleasantly surprised.

Grab Snacks

The combination of raw unsalted nuts or seeds and a piece of fruit is perfect for a boost of energy mid-morning. Eating the protein in the nuts or seeds at the same time as the fruit helps to slow down the release of the fruit's natural sugars, ensuring that energy levels stay tip-top and blood sugar levels stable. These kinds of snacks are also very convenient, great for eating on the go and will help prevent the crisp and chocolate cravings that we all get from time to time.

Choose local, seasonal fruit where possible. Domestic fruits such as apples, pears and berries (strawberries, raspberries and blueberries) are lower in sugar than the more exotic fruits – and the fresher (and less travelled) they are, the richer the nutrient content. As well as being an excellent source of protein, nuts and seeds are a fantastic source of essential 'good' fats that are vital for optimal brain function and healthy hair, nails and skin.

Nuts and seeds have a bad reputation for being filled with calories. They are in fact filled with goodness – but as with most things, too much of a good thing can often be bad. So for this mid-morning snack, use the 'rule of palm' approach: eat only the amount of nuts or seeds that fits neatly into the palm of your hand (about 15–20g). You will find that when you buy a bag of nuts or seeds in the shops it will be a lot more than 20g, so don't be tempted to scoff the lot.

Our recommended combinations of fruit with raw nuts or seeds are listed opposite, but feel free to experiment. We recommend combining 100–120g of fruit with 15–20g of nuts or seeds.

1	Black Grapes & Pecans
2	Pear & Sunflower Seeds
3	Fresh Figs
4	Pineapple & Sesame Seeds
5	Satsuma & Cashew Nuts
6	Apple & Almonds
7	Stone Fruit & Sunflower Seeds
8	Pear & Pumpkin Seeds
9	Banana & Cashew Nuts
10	Papaya & Sesame Seeds
11	Stone Fruit & Brazil Nuts
12	Apple & Sunflower Seeds
13	Kiwi & Hazelnuts
14	Mango & Sesame Seeds
15	Berries & Almonds
16	Black Grapes & Sunflower Seeds
17	Pineapple & Hazelnuts
18	Stone Fruit & Almonds
19	Satsuma & Pistachio Nuts
20	Tangerine & Pumpkin Seeds
21	Berries & Brazil Nuts

THE THREE-WEEK PLAN

The Three-Week Plan

AS YOU HAVE PROBABLY REALISED, I AM A BIG PLANNER when it comes to eating the right food, and my recipe book wouldn't be complete without giving you the necessary guidelines to eat a perfectly balanced diet. Eating healthily can be something that becomes part of your daily routine and this plan has been created so you can do just that.

The three-week plan includes most of the recipes in this book (we have given you a few extra to enjoy too) and I hope it will help those of you who find this way of eating completely different to what you have become accustomed to.

Each day has been carefully analysed so that it is balanced with the correct amount of carbohydrates (fruit, vegetables, complex carbohydrates), proteins (cheese, meat, poultry, pulses) and essential fats (nuts, seeds, oily fish) and contains everything your body needs to function optimally.

A few tips for your own planning:

- Spread your ingredients out. For example, don't have all the chicken-based dishes one after the other.
- Make sure you eat a source of essential fats every day.
- Plan ahead. Buy suitable containers for your lunch and snacks, especially if eating at work or on the go.
- Eat a balance of protein and carbohydrates in each meal (see the rule of palm, page 15)
- Make sure you eat around five to eight portions of fruit and vegetables a day (government guidelines recommend 80g per portion). This doesn't include starchy vegetables such as potatoes.

A good plan is also a flexible one. It needs to work for you, and your current lifestyle. Feel free to mix and match as you see fit. Leftovers from a dinner could be used as lunch for the following day with a salad, and a number of easy- and quick-to-make snacks can be used as a lunch on the go.

Obviously, being healthy is all about balance, so you will find there are a few treats thrown in there too. Here's to wishing you the best of health.

Week 1

DAY	BREAKFAST	LUNCH	DINNER	SNACK	GRAB SNACK
MON	Apple & Blackberry Porridge 35	Crab, Chilli & Rocket Salad 103	Paneer Cheese with Masala Spinach 130	Cinnamon Spiced Plums 198	Black Grapes & Pecans 207
TUE	Raw Cashew Nut Butter 49	Spiced Pearl Spelt, Goat's Cheese & Walnut Salad 95	Crispy Sea Bass Tagine with Coriander Couscous 149	Lemon & Coriander Hummus with Carrot Sticks 172	Pear & Sunflower Seeds 207
WED	Mango & Granola Muesli 32	Chicken Superfood Salad 80	Wild Mushroom Barley Risotto 117	Ginger Infused Fruit & Seed Salad 185	Fresh Figs 207
THU	Poached Eggs with Wilted Spinach & Feta Cheese 50	Puy Lentil & Salmon Salad 104	Pesto Chicken with Roasted Vegetables 125	Baba Ganoush with Oatcakes 182	Pineapple & Sesame Seeds 207
FRI	Banana & Berry Bircher Muesli 42	Thai Chicken Noodle Salad 72	Mexican Bean Pot 133	Chocolate Mousse 202	Satsuma & Cashew Nuts 207
SAT	Bubble & Squeak with Smoked Salmon 54	Feta & Herb Lentil Salad 100	Turmeric Chicken with Spicy Tomato Aubergine 118	Fresh Spring Rolls with Sweet Chilli Sauce 165	Apple & Almonds 207
SUN	Papaya & Granola Muesli 32	Lightly Spiced Beetroot & Coconut Soup 67	Roast Beef with Home-made Horseradish Sauce 157	Banana, Date & Apricot Muffins 205	Stone Fruit & Sunflower Seeds 207

Week 2

DAY	BREAKFAST	LUNCH	DINNER	SNACK	GRAB SNACK
MON	Strawberry & Mango Bircher Muesli 45	Smoked Venison Salad 92	Spiced Coconut Prawns with Roasted Cherry Tomatoes 121	Roasted Red Pepper Hummus with Celery & Radishes 170	Pear & Pumpkin Seeds 207
TUE	Bubble & Squeak with Poached Eggs 53	Niçoise Salad 83	Duck & Pearl Barley Cassoulet with Honey & Caraway Parsnips 154	Stewed Spiced Apple Yoghurt 197	Berries & Brazil Nuts 207
WED	Pineapple & Granola Muesli 32	Spiced Butternut & Couscous Salad with Raspberry Vinaigrette 75	Chicken & Noodle Laksa 114	Baked Stone Fruit with Ricotta 201	Papaya & Sesame Seeds 207
THU	Baby Spinach & Ricotta Omelette 56	Salmon & Dill Terrine 76	Sea Bream with Mint Pesto 122	Tomato Salsa with Corn Chips 178	Stone Fruit & Brazil Nuts 207
FRI	Seasonal Fruit and Granola Muesli 32	Warm Teriyaki Chicken Salad 87	Roasted Red Peppers with St Tola Log 129	Chocolate Mousse with Raspberries 202	Apple & Sunflower Seeds 207
SAT	Cardamom Spiced Kedgeree with Poached Quail's Eggs 59	Wasabi Brown Rice & Soya Bean Salad 99	Dhal with a Cinnamon Spiced Mushroom Pilaf 146	Stewed Fig Yoghurt 194	Kiwi & Hazelnuts 207
SUN	Lime, Banana & Cashew Nut Granola Pot 39	Thai Broth with Prawns & Noodles 64	Chicken, Feta & Leek Pie 153	Rhubarb & Ginger Jelly 186	Mango & Sesame Seeds 207

Week 3

DAY	BREAKFAST	LUNCH	DINNER	SNACK	GRAB SNACK
MON	Pear & Blackberry Bircher Muesli 43	Roasted Vegetable & Feta Salad 84	Griddled Kingfish Thai Green Curry 138	Pea & Avocado Guacamole 181	Banana & Cashew Nuts 207
TUE	Melon & Raspberry Granola Muesli 32	Gado Gado Salad 79	Chicken & Prawn Pad Thai 145	Stewed Plum Yoghurt 190	Black Grapes & Sunflower Seeds 207
WED	Pistachio Butter on Rye & Grapefruit 49	Sweet Potato, Beetroot & Tymsboro Goat's Cheese Salad 88	Miso Red Snapper with Asian Vegetables 134	Hummus with Corn Chips 169	Pineapple & Hazelnuts 207
THU	Wild Rice, Coconut & Mango Bircher 38	Smoked Trout Pâté with Toasted Rye Bread & Carrot Salad 71	Cottage Pie with Baby Potato & Goat's Cheese Mash 150	Stewed Pears with Coconut Yoghurt 193	Stone Fruit & Almonds 207
FRI	Banana & Sultana Bircher Muesli 41	Goat's Cheese, Sun-dried Tomato & Lamb's Lettuce Salad 96	Pumpkin & Peanut Curry 126	Chocolate Mousse with Hazelnuts 202	Berries & Almonds 207
SAT	Oat Pancakes with Fruit & Vanilla Yoghurt 46	Chicken with Coconut Noodles & Asian Coleslaw 108	Feta Stuffed Butternut Squash 142	Artichoke & Bean Dip with Sugar Snap Peas 174	Tangerine & Pumpkin Seeds 207
SUN	Vanilla, Prune & Pecan Pot 36	Pea, Feta & Scallop Soup 68	Gaby's Garlic & Ginger Chicken 141	Summer Pudding Jelly with Vanilla & Honey Greek Yoghurt 189	Satsuma & Pistachio Nuts 207

GLOSSARY OF INGREDIENTS

This is not intended to be an encyclopaedia, more of a helping hand (with some interesting trivia thrown in) to find the ingredients listed in our recipes. To us, they are all commonly used foods – but when we asked our friends to test the recipes we quickly realised that others just didn't know what they are or where to find them. I hope this helps.

agar-agar
A vegetarian alternative to gelatine, agar-agar is derived from seaweed. Known as 'Kanten' in Japanese or 'Falooda' in Indian, it is traditionally used to set oriental desserts. It can be found in some specialist shops, and online at The Asian Cookshop (www.theasiancookshop.co.uk) or Wai Yee Hong (www.waiyeehong.com). You can use VegeSet or gelatine if you prefer.

alfalfa sprouts
Alfalfa is a purple flowering plant in the pea family. The young shoots, eaten within 4–7 days of germination, are popular in the health-food industry due to their rich nutrient content. They have a delicate flavour and make a great addition to salads and open sandwiches. They can be found in some large supermarkets (in the salad aisle). Substitute sprouted mung beans, sprouted peas or sprouted sunflower seeds if alfalfa sprouts are not available.

artichoke hearts
Low in calories and rich in vitamin C, folate and potassium, globe artichokes are thought to come from north Africa, where they still grow wild. They are delicious, but can be expensive to buy fresh and difficult to prepare at home, so we recommend buying artichoke hearts ready-prepared and preserved in oil. Sometimes also called 'artichoke antipasti', you can find them in all good supermarkets, either in a jar or on the deli counter (with the olives).

black sesame seeds
Rich in copper and manganese, sesame seeds have a nutty flavour and add a delicate crunch to Asian dishes. We love the black ones as they really enhance the appearance of a dish, but they can be tricky to find. Try The Asian Cookshop (www.theasiancookshop.co.uk) or Wai Yee Hong (www.waiyeehong.com) – or use white sesame seeds, which are widely available.

barley couscous
Couscous is normally made from wheat, but we prefer barley couscous (traditional in certain parts of Morocco) due to its lower GI (see page 18). Belazu is the most common brand of barley couscous and can be found in larger Sainsbury's and Waitrose stores or online.

barley flakes
Processed from pearl barley, barley flakes look like oats and can usually be found at health-food shops, or online at Holland & Barrett (www.hollandandbarrett.com).

bouquet garni
This is a bundle of herbs used to season food during cooking, and removed before serving. Traditionally it is tied with string (if you want to make your own, we suggest a combination of fresh parsley, thyme and bay leaves), but ready-made bouquets garnis are wrapped in mesh or even in teabag-like sachets. They are stocked with the spices in most supermarkets.

brown rice flour
A great gluten-free alternative to standard (wheat) brown flour. It is available from larger supermarkets and online from Sharpham Park (www.sharphampark.com).

brown rice puffs
Also called puffed rice, these are available from larger supermarkets, and usually found in the breakfast cereals aisle. They do not always list 'brown' in the name – but you can check the ingredients to ensure that you are getting wholegrain brown rice.

brown rice vinegar
This mild, slightly sweet Japanese vinegar is sold in Asian supermarkets. It is also sometimes called 'rice wine vinegar' – but it is made from rice, not rice wine. You can substitute white rice vinegar (available in most supermarkets) or cider vinegar, which is widely available.

caraway seeds
Common in European cuisine, caraway seeds are not actually seeds! They are the split halves of the dried fruit. You can find them in the spices aisle of most supermarkets – but if they are unavailable, fennel seeds make a good alternative.

cardamom pods	An Indian spice and part of the ginger family, cardamom has a distinctive and relatively strong flavour. It is stocked in the spices aisle of supermarkets. We prefer using the pods, but you can buy ground cardamom too.
cavolo nero	Used a lot in Italian cooking (it is a traditional ingredient in minestrone) it is also known as Tuscan kale and has a slightly sweeter taste than curly kale. It can be quite tricky to get hold of, but other greens or curly kale are a good substitute.
coconut flakes	Coconuts are one of the only nuts you can toast without the heat converting good fats to bad. These flakes (also known as flaked coconut) have a nicer texture than dessicated coconut and can be found in good health-food shops.
enoki mushrooms	Enoki (or enokitake) are long, thin Japanese mushrooms used in Asian cuisine, traditionally in soups. They are also yummy served raw in salads and add a stunning garnish. They can often be found at farmers' markets or good greengrocers, and are occasionally stocked in larger supermarkets, usually in a mixed packet of 'speciality mushrooms'. They can be replaced with another type of mushroom if unavailable.
fenugreek powder	Raw fenugreek seeds (called Methi in India) are thought to have a therapeutic and healing effect on joint pains. The powder is widely used in Indian cuisine and can be found in the spices aisle of the supermarket.
five spice powder	Based on the Chinese philosophy of balancing the yin and yang of food, this Chinese mix of five spices (also known as Chinese five spice) is traditionally made up of cloves, cinnamon, star anise, fennel and ginger. It is stocked in the spices aisle of the supermarket. It's important to read the ingredients before using in sweet dishes as a number of brands add salt, pepper and other savoury ingredients to their mix.
garam masala	Meaning 'hot mixture' in Hindi, garam masala is traditionally a regional or house mix of spices. For that reason, different brands contain different spices – but any one will do. It is stocked in the spices aisle of the supermarket.
Golden Cross	An unpasteurised goat's milk cheese made by Kevin and Alison Blunt in Sussex. It is very pretty when cut because the ash rind gives a nice ring that almost makes it look like a slice of fish. It is made with vegetarian rennet. If you cannot get a hold of it, substitute another full-flavoured goat's cheese.
groundnut oil	This is the only oil that we use to cook with. It has a very high smoking point (230ºC compared to olive oil's 190ºC), making it more stable and therefore more beneficial to health. It is available in most supermarkets.
horseradish	The horseradish root can often be found growing along roadsides and canal towpaths if you know what you're looking for. If not, ask your greengrocer or shop for it at farmers' markets. Fresh horseradish root can be frozen (and grated from frozen, so there's no need to defrost). If peeling onions makes you cry, you haven't lived yet! Horseradish is mighty strong and if you're a wuss you might want to put on swimming goggles when grating it or buy it grated in a jar from the shops. Do check what's in the jar, though – the table-ready horseradish sauce that is sold in supermarkets usually contains a very small proportion of horseradish along with a variety of ingredients which might include oil, vinegar, eggs, cream, sugar, salt and preservatives, and is a poor substitute for the real thing.
kaffir lime leaves	Used primarily in Southeast Asian cuisine, lime leaves add a lovely, aromatic, citrussy flavour to sauces. They can be found dried in most supermarkets, in the herbs and spices aisle.

kingfish	A big game fish and part of the mackerel family, kingfish is an oily fish with a relatively light flavour, normally served as steaks. High-street fishmongers rarely have it, but try buying online from The Fish Society (www.thefishsociety.co.uk) or Good Taste Foods (www.goodtastefoods.co.uk). You can substitute a white fish such as sea bream or snapper, or another oily fish, if you wish.
lamb's lettuce	Also occasionally known as corn salad or mache, this soft leaf is available in most supermarkets as a bagged salad leaf.
lemongrass	Native to the Philippines, where it is used in teas and curries, lemongrass has a fantastic aroma and adds that special something to Asian dishes. It is available in the fresh herbs and spices section of larger supermarkets, or in Asian supermarkets. Its oil is also used as an insect repellent (known as citronella) to keep the mozzies away!
linseeds	Also known as flax seeds, linseeds are a fantastic source of essential fats. In fact, they are so good for you that you can even buy linseed powder to sprinkle on your food for added goodness. The seeds can usually be found in the baking section of larger supermarkets with the dried fruit and nuts, or they are are easily available in health-food shops.
maize meal	This is simply a flour ground from dried maize (corn). It can usually be found in health food shops or online from Holland & Barrett (www.hollandandbarrett.com).
millet flakes	Interestingly, millet (not rice) formed an important part of the prehistoric diet in India and China. It is a great gluten-free alternative to wheat flakes and can usually be found in health-food shops or online from Holland & Barrett (www.hollandandbarrett.com).
millet grain	Like millet flakes, the grain can usually be found in health-food shops or online from Holland & Barrett (www.hollandandbarrett.com).
mirin	A Japanese rice wine, similar to sake but with a lower alcohol content, mirin is used in a number of our Asian dressings and stir-fries. It can usually be found in the world food section of larger supermarkets. If you can't find it you can substitute sake (found in the spirits aisle), but we recommend you cook off some of the alcohol first.
miso paste	Miso is a thick Japanese seasoning made from fermenting either soya beans, brown rice or barley. It can be found in the world foods section of larger supermarkets. For gluten-free diets, stick to miso made from brown rice or soya beans.
mizuna	Meaning 'water greens' in Japanese, this leaf is slightly peppery in flavour (but not as pungent as rocket) and is great in Asian-influenced salads and stir-fries. It can be found in Asian supermarkets, or at good greengrocers and farmers' markets.
oyster mushrooms	Although they were first cultivated in Germany, oyster mushrooms are now more widely used in Asian cuisine. They are available in the fresh produce section of larger supermarkets. If you can't find them, chestnut mushrooms are readily available and have a nice flavour.
pad Thai rice noodles	Traditional pad Thai noodles are available in Asian supermarkets, online at The Asian Cookshop (www.theasiancookshop.co.uk), or in some larger supermarkets. If you can't find them, use wide flat rice noodles, which is basically what they are – ideally they should be 1cm wide.
pak choi	Sometimes known as bok choy, this Chinese cabbage can be found in larger supermarkets or Asian supermarkets. You can substitute pointed cabbage, which is more readily available.
paneer	An Indian cheese that does not require rennet, making it completely vegetarian, paneer is rubbery in texture, so always chop it small and use it in spiced and flavoursome dishes only. It is usually available in the cheese section of larger supermarkets.

pearl barley	We use this a lot instead of risotto rice as its GI is much lower (see page 18). It has fantastic bite and is great in salads too. It can be found in larger supermarkets or health-food shops.
pearl spelt	Similar in texture, look and taste to pearl barley, pearl spelt can be difficult to find. We suggest buying it from Sharpham Park (www.sharphampark.com).
porcini mushrooms	Commonly bought dried, we use these as they have a great depth of flavour. They are available in most supermarkets.
Puy lentils	Named after the region in France in which they are grown, these green lentils (actually they are almost black in colour) are high in protein and low in carbs. They can usually be found in larger supermarkets or health-food shops. They are occasionally known as French lentils, and can be replaced with green or brown lentils if Puy can't be found.
quail's eggs	These tiny eggs, which taste much like hens' eggs, can often be found in larger supermarkets, farmers' markets or greengrocers. Cooked quail's eggs are also available in a jar.
quinoa	A South American grain which can be used in place of rice or potatoes, quinoa has a nutty flavour and texture. It can usually be found in larger supermarkets; otherwise buy it in health-food shops or online from Holland & Barrett (www.hollandandbarrett.com).
radicchio	Related to chicory, radicchio is pink-red in colour and has a bitter taste. It can be found at greengrocers and farmers' markets or grown at home, but it is rarely seen in the supermarkets unless it's in a mixed bag of salad.
Ragstone	An unpasteurised goat's milk cheese made in Herefordshire, Ragstone has a warm taste and a smooth texture. It is made with traditional animal rennet so if you are vegetarian you may want to use an alternative.
red chard	Another salad leaf that is sometimes found in a mixed salad bag, red chard can sometimes be found in bigger quantities at greengrocers or farmers' markets, or grown at home.
red lentils	Beautiful in colour, these can really spruce up a dish and can usually be found in supermarkets. They are sometimes known as red split peas.
rice flour pancakes	We use these to wrap our spring rolls. They are a great storecupboard ingredient as they come in packs of around 200 and keep for ages! You can buy them from Asian supermarkets or online from The Asian Cookshop (www.theasiancookshop.co.uk).
rose harissa	A hot Tunisian paste made from chillies, oil and rose petals, rose harissa is slightly smoky in flavour. The most readily available brand is Belazu, which is stocked by larger branches of Sainsbury's and Waitrose. It is usually stocked in the the 'specialist ingredients' or spices aisle.
rye bread	Rye gives a rich, dense loaf that is high in fibre. We recommend buying one that is made of 100 per cent rye, as many loaves of 'rye bread' have wheat flour mixed into the dough.
sesame oil	This nutty oil adds a lovely subtle flavour to Asian dishes. Mainly used in salads, it is usually stocked with the oils in good supermarkets.
shiitake mushrooms	Great in Asian dishes, shiitake mushrooms have a rubbery texture that lends itself well to sautéeing, but they are less good raw or roasted. Usually available in the fresh produce section of larger supermarkets – but if you can't find them, substitute chestnut mushrooms.
smoked venison	A delicious meat! Some supermarkets stock smoked venison, or you can order it from The Pure Package's supplier, Upton Smokery (www.uptonsmokery.co.uk).
soya beans	Rich in protein, and the only vegetable to contain all eight essential amino acids (page 20), these can usually be found in the freezer section of larger supermarkets.

soya bran	With similar health benefits to soya beans, in a different form, this is available from health-food shops.
sprouted peas	Like alfalfa sprouts, sprouted peas make a great addition to salads and open sandwiches and have a delicate flavour. They also look great as a garnish, and are becoming more readily available in larger supermarkets. Substitute other sprouts if you can't find them.
star anise	Used mainly in Chinese, Malaysian and Indian cooking, star anise gives a light aniseed flavour. We mainly use it when roasting or poaching fruit. It is stocked with the spices in most supermarkets.
tahini	A sesame seed paste used as the base of Mediterranean and Middle Eastern salads and dips (it is a key ingredient in hummus), tahini can usually be found in the world foods section of larger supermarkets or in health-food shops.
tilapia	This fast-growing fish is now widely farmed and can increasingly be found either whole or filleted on the fresh fish counter in supermarkets. It is also available from local fishmongers.
tamari soy sauce	Tamari is thicker and darker than regular soy sauce, and is slightly smoky in flavour. Derived from fermented soya beans (miso paste), it is naturally gluten free.
Thai fish sauce	Often just called fish sauce, or alternatively known by its Thai name, 'nam pla', this is available in the world foods section of most good supermarkets.
Tymsboro	An unpasteurised goat's milk cheese made by Mary Holbrook in Somerset, Tymsboro has an interesting shape and each one looks unique because of the effect of the mould growing in the ash coating. It is make with animal rennet so if you are a vegetarian you may want to substitute a different cheese.
St Tola	An unpasteurised goat's milk cheese from County Clare, a stunning place in the west of Ireland. This cheese is made by Siobhan Ni Ghairbith using traditional animal rennet. It is a log-shaped cheese not dissimilar to French chèvre. If you are unable to find St Tola then this recipe works well with chèvre, which is of similar dimensions – they both sit nicely on top of the pepper.
vanilla paste	Available online from Little Pod (http://littlepod.co.uk/), this paste in our opinion really is the best, and it is worth buying some and just keeping it in your cupboard. If you can't find it, the seeds from one vanilla pod can be used to substitute 1 teaspoon of paste. Of course, if you want you can use vanilla extract, but it really doesn't do vanilla justice.
VegeSet	This is the vegetarian gelling agent we use at The Pure Package. You can buy it online from Just Whole Foods (www.justwholefoods.co.uk), or substitute agar-agar or gelatine if you prefer.
vermicelli rice noodles	Also sometimes called fine rice noodles. It seems a lot of supermarkets have stopped stocking the dried varieties, so we recommend you buy them online from The Asian Cookshop (www.theasiancookshop.co.uk). Some supermarkets do stock fresh varieties, but these often have added oils and preservatives – making them our last choice.
wasabi paste	This fiery horseradish paste is often served with sushi. It can usually be found in the world foods section of larger supermarkets. Powdered versions are often easier to get hold of, in which case just follow the packet instructions to make the paste.
wild rice	Black in colour, wild rice is high in protein and fibre and it is a great alternative to brown rice or other grains. It is available in some larger supermarkets, stocked either alongside the rice or with the specialist grains. We recommend the quick-cook version in this book for ease, but some supermarkets may only stock the regular version, so be sure to look at the packet instructions for recommended cooking times before diving into our recipes.
Worcestershire sauce	A liquid condiment usually containing anchovies and primarily used to season meat, Worcestershire sauce is stocked with the condiments and table sauces in most supermarkets.

INDEX

Acknowledgements

AS A WIFE AND MOTHER I could not have achieved anything if it was not for the
people around me. I am surrounded by an amazing support group and the most key
person in this is Gaby Melvin. She has been my rock, when having babies and busily
writing this book, Gaby has made sure The Pure Package has been running perfectly.
Many recipes in this book are inspired by her travels and experiences and also those
of Kevin Bryant and Ulrika Saba.

My parents have been a huge inspiration for me, and continue to be. It is only now how
much I appreciate my mother's hard work bringing up children whilst establishing her
pioneering cheese company, Milleens. My father taught me to have respect for food,
where it comes from, the importance of animal welfare and most of all the love of food.

I would like to thank my husband Stephen Irvine for being patient when I have been
busy testing recipes. To my nanny Elizabeth Reyes for making sure I did not feel guilty
for spending time away from my kids when writing this book. I know they are happy.
To Lovely Zamora for tirelessly testing recipes with incredible attention to detail
and Victoria Cleary-Ford who has over the last six years made sure my recipes are
nutritionally balanced – and I thank her for not being a complete food Nazi.

I especially want to thank the whole team at The Pure Package, who are consistently
loyal and do a great job, especially my assistant Rachel O'Connell. A special thanks
to my suppliers and farmers, who produce the wonderful ingredients that we use at
The Pure Package: I thank them for the constant supply of high-quality produce that
we receive.

I would like to say a big thank you to all who have contributed to the making of this
book, especially my agent Clare Hulton for your trusted direction and everyone at Orion,
in particular to our publisher Amanda Harris and Natasha Webber for their guidance and
constant support. A huge part of a recipe book coming to life is the photography of our
precious recipes, so I would like to thank Jean Cazals for producing beautiful images that
truly bring the recipes to life. Thanks also to our stylist and home economists Cynthia
Inions, Katie Giovanni, Megan Rogers and Julia Azzarello for the creative styling.

Finally, I would like to thank each and every Pure Package client, who have continued
to enjoy our food and use our service faithfully, without whom this book would never
have been written.

Jennifer Irvine